the BEST Of Aussie SLaNG

by
Eric Spilsted

Designed by
Melinda Vassallo
Illustrated by
Paul Gearside with
Vaughan Campbell

Published by Eric Spilsted Publishing
111 Ernest Street, Crows Nest. NSW Australia.

ISBN 0 -9577725 2 1
First published 2003
Printed in Australia by McPhersons Printing Group

ConTENts

About the author

Born in Sydney, **Eric Spilsted** grew up in the Riverina town of Junee where in shearing sheds and railway yards he had his first contact with real Aussie language.

He spent most of his working life in advertising and currently runs his own publishing business specialising in rugby **football** publications including the weekly publication *Rugby News*.

In many years of **knocking** around lots of good and bad places, he has compiled this **fascinating** collection of Aussie words and phrases which form part of the Australian **way of life.**

Gidday!

So youse want to LEARN to

understand

(or even speak) AUSSie.

Well this little

book will get you started.

We've given you a whole

bunch of everyday Aussie

words like

chooks and DUNNY.

Australia
It's a funny sort of a place.

A place where the **crows fly backwards to keep the sun out of their eyes.**

We call friends and strangers **'mate'** This can be traced to the harsh conditions on the Australian frontier in the early part of the last century and the development of mutual aid.

Or perhaps it's just because we're hopeless with names.

We have a highly developed sense of humour that borders on irreverence and a general distrust of authority. Perhaps that's a reflection of our convict background.

We love sport, the beach and the barbecue. At Xmas time we maintain our ancestral traditions by having large hot meals and plum puddings in stinking hot temperatures.

There is no Australian event which cannot be improved by a **sausage sizzle** and that there's no food that cannot be improved by a liberal application of **dead horse** (tomato sauce)

We have a lot of **'sickies'** – paid leave from work due to illness. We spend these days playing golf, at the cricket, or on the beach.

On picnics we take an icebox called an **Esky**. The Esky is always too small for both food and beer so we leave most of the food at home.

Aussie Slang

Aussie slang is clever, colourful, funny and mostly irreverent.

Much of this **sub-language** evolved in the Australian outback. It moved to the cities through the Depression, two world wars, **post-war immigration** and the **yuppie emergence.**

Some words have come and gone, many remain in use and new words and phrases are constantly emerging. Listed here are the more popular expressions used by a wide range of Aussies.

There is a preoccupation with **drinking, gambling, body parts** and **fornication**, but like it or not, that's what people talk about.

Phrases such as dry as a dead dingo's donger, flat out like a lizard drinking and **up shit creek without a paddle**, create vivid word pictures not easily achieved with conventional language.

The Best of Aussie Slang is for those who want to colour their speech or just be reminded of the unique, whimsical and fun way that Aussies talk to and about each other.

Try a few in your **conversation**. Your friends will either be amazed, amused or perhaps will no longer be your friends!

typical Aussie characters

We have created a series of **typical** Aussie characters who represent the types of people who would be likely to colour their conversation with sprinklings of classic Aussie slang and rhyming slang. You'll hear them all wherever you go throughout Australia.

John - our hero

He's just an average bloke.
Around 35 to 45 years old,
average height and weight,
average clothing and hair style,
probably has a wife and 2.5 kids,
has a mortgage, works in an average
job and likes a few beers with his
mates.
He enjoys watching rugby, cricket
and AFL and is not over-ambitious.
Just a nice average bloke who is
mostly good but sometimes naughty.

Harry - the punter

Harry is a somewhat smallish man in his 40's or 50's who can be found around the pubs and racecourses of Australia.

He is a sharp dresser who often has the mandatory pair of field glasses slung around his neck.

He wears a snappy 'pork pie' hat and rather loud suits.

He is very streetwise and knows a lot of people. They are mostly trainers, jockeys, petty criminals and barmaids.

Harry may be married, but one would never know. He has no interests other than horse racing and drinking at his favourite watering hole.

Mick - the truckie

Mick is a large man. He always wears a blue singlet, shorts and thongs and is liberally tattooed.

He is a hard man who played football and knows how to handle himself in a fight.

He is however good natured and never gets drunk despite the fact that he consumes enormous quantities of dark beer.

Tim - the yuppie

Tim is 25 - 35 years old. He dresses in the latest fashions, has a styled hairdo, works in advertising, merchant banking, IT or foreign exchange. He is often talking on a mobile phone and always frequents the trendiest of bars where he drinks chardonnay. He lives in Paddington or Carlton, is single and is preoccupied with his appearance and his next date.

Jack - the bushie

He's tall, thin and has gaunt features. He comes from somewhere up the scrub and has done a bit of everything. He likes a drink and a chat and is very relaxed and easy going. He speaks with a drawl and wears a broad-brimmed hat which is often surrounded by flies.

Sheila - the girl

She's just your average fun-loving Aussie girl. She is reasonably tall, wears tight skirts and has big tits. She doesn't have a special man, she enjoys a few beers with the blokes and is regarded by all as a 'good sport.'

GREAT Aussie Words

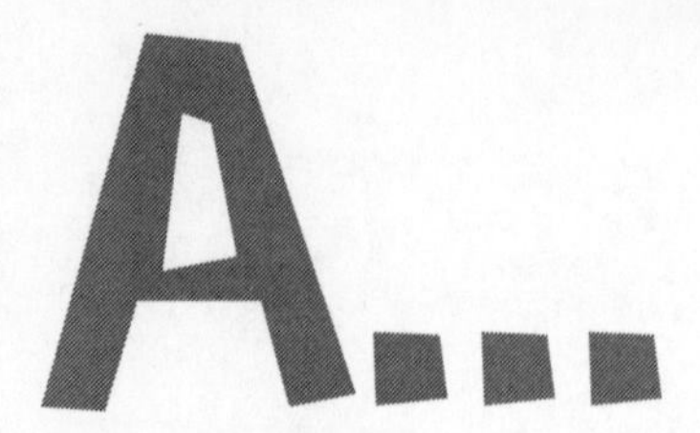

angle of the dangle An erection

It's a well-known principle that the angle of the dangle is proportionate to the seriousness of the erection. If the erection is on the way or less than successful, it may be classified as half a...

Alternatives to describe this happy state are:
bar
brute
fat (crack a)
hard-on
horn (crack a)
larrikin's hat (fat)
mongrel
morning glory
Sarah Vaughan (horn)
woodie

ankle-biter A small child

'Mum went to town and took the ankle-biters.'
Some prefer **rug-rat**.

anotherie Another one - usually more beer.
'Let's have anotherie' or 'let's have a coldie.'

ape-shit Very angry - 'he went ape-shit when I told him.'

apples 'She's apples'
- everything's fine and in good order.

arse Rear end, bum
Arse may be used to describe the bums of both sexes. The options below usually describe a man's bum although there's no hard-and-fast rule.
acre
arsehole (also describes people)
bracket
clacker
coit
coke hole
date
deaf and dumb (bum)
dinger
freckle
Gary Glitter (shitter) (Gary)
Jon Voight (coit)
Khyber (Pass)
ring
tan track
Tijuana Brass

Other uses of arse

arse-about-face
- something that is back-to-front or '**arse-up**.'

arse beats class - luck often wins over ability.

arse out of his pants - down and out.

arse over head/tit - falling over.
'He went arse over tit' or 'base over apex'.

fart-arse - wasting time on useless pursuits.
'He's always fart-arsing around.'

get off your arse or
get your arse into gear - get busy.

get the arse/boot
- get fired.

make an arse of yourself
- to screw up badly.

more arse than Jessie - unusually good luck.
Jessie was a famous Sydney Zoo elephant.
Sometimes - 'he's very arsey.'

pain in the arse - an annoying person.
'He's a real pain in the arse.'

piece of arse - a woman.
'I got a piece of arse' - sexual success.

short-arse - a vertically-challenged person.

smartarse - a boring know-all.

tight-arse - a mean, miserly person.

tin-arse - lucky.
'He's a real tin-arse' or 'he's tinny.'

ball & chain Wife
Used by blokes when talking about their wives, never when talking to them.
Handbrake or **war office** are popular alternatives.

bag To 'bag' someone is to disparage or knock them.
Bag your head! - a strong statement of disagreement.
Old bag - a woman who is past her prime.
In the bag - the desired result is now certain.

balls Testicles
Other useful options include:
agates
bollocks
cluster
cods
family/crown jewels
goolies
Jatz Crackers (knackers)
Niagara Falls (Niagaras)
nuts
orchestra stalls (orchestras)
town halls

balls-and-all Enthusiastic involvement, considering what's at stake - 'I'll be in that balls-and-all.'

ball-tearer Someone or something with exceptionally good qualities
- 'the game was a real ball-tearer.'

balls-up When everything goes wrong
- 'it's a proper balls-up.' Some prefer stuff-up, cock-up, screw-up or fuck-up.

bangers Sausages - ordered as bangers and mash.

bar 'I won't have a bar of him' - to choose to have nothing to do with someone.
'I'm getting a bar' - an erection.

barrack Vigorous support for the team
- 'I barrack for Sydney.'
Curiously, Americans root for their teams.

bash To have a bash (or burl) at something is to make an attempt at the task - 'I'll give it a bash.'
A party - 'it was a great bash.'

bastard A popular Aussie word which is rarely used to suggest illegitimacy and often used as a term of friendship.
'Owyagoin, you old bastard?' - friendly
'He's not a bad bastard' - good
'He's a poor bastard' - unfortunate
'He's a rotten bastard' - bad
'He's a silly bastard' - stupid

basket case Someone who has serious mental problems.
Other less serious options are:
a fruit cake
a screw loose
around the twist/bend
away with the fairies/pixies
gone ga-ga
in cuckoo land
lost the plot
not the full quid

battery acid Cheap white wine in cardboard casks

battler One who struggles for a livelihood - 'he's a real battler.'

beak A judge or magistrate.
One fronts or fronts-up to the beak.

beeline A direct course - 'he made a beeline for the pub.'

belly-up When a business goes broke, it goes belly-up. The same for people who depart the scene permanently.

belter Very good - 'the game was a real belter.'

bible-basher An excessively religious person

bickies Large sums of money - 'the house is for sale but they're talking big bickies.'

big-note One who is boastful and likes to exaggerate his achievements is called a big-noter.

bike To 'get off your bike' is to become angry and lose control. The **town bike** is a sexually promiscuous female - everybody gets a ride.

bingle A car crash. Most prefer to have a 'prang.'

blind Freddie An imaginary character who represents a high degree of incompetence - 'the answer is so obvious that even blind Freddie could see it.'

bloke Aussie men are called blokes. They're mostly good blokes.

bloodhouse A hotel whose patrons are given to riotous behaviour - 'that place is a real bloodhouse.'

bloody The great Aussie adjective. Can be used to add emphasis to most words and usually is - bloody good, bloody awful, bloody anything.

blow misfortune -'what a blow.'
blow-in – an unexpected guest.
blow job – oral sex
blow through – to leave the scene.
blow your dough – to lose your money.
blow the whistle – to inform on someone.
blow up/blow your top – to lose control.

blower Telephone - 'he's on the blower.'

bludger Someone who is lazy and doesn't pull his weight - thus the term dole bludger.

blue A fight - 'he bunged on a blue in the pub.'
A dispute - 'I'm blueing with him.'
A mistake - 'I made a real blue.'
Sudden and unexpected - out of the blue.
A red-headed man is called 'Bluey.'

boat race A rigged horse race
- 'It's a boat race in the third.'
Also a teams drinking contest often held at rugby after-match functions.

bog To 'go for a bog' is to defecate.
Also another name for a dunny
- 'I'm going to the bog.'

bog in To start eating - 'let's bog in.'

boiler Usually an 'old boiler' - an old and unattractive woman. Alternative is **'old crow.'**

bollocky Nude - 'she's in the bollocky.'
Also - in the nuddy or starkers.

bolter A long-odds winner - usually a horse.

boobs Breasts
Women prefer to have boobs and only men use alternatives to describe those pointy bits.
brace and bits (tits)
Brad Pitts (tits)
Bristol cities (titties)
each way bet (set)
Eartha Kitts (tits)
fun bags
jugs
knockers
norks

boofhead A very stupid person

booze All alcohol
You buy your booze, have a booze-up and try to avoid the booze bus on the way home.
The booze bus is a police bus used for the breath testing of motorists.

bo-peep To look - 'have a bo-peep at this.'

brass razoo To not have a brass razoo is to be very down-and-out financially.
A razoo is an old term for a gambling chip.

brewers droop Flaccidity
When the angle-of-the-dangle is related conversely to the volume of alcohol drunk.

broke Seriously short of money.
Stony broke or skint is even more serious.
To 'go for broke' is to throw caution to the wind - 'we're now in deep shit, so let's go for broke.'

brown-eye Bum-baring in public as a gesture of contempt or simply for amusement.
Also known as **mooning**.

brown-nose To brown-nose is to suck-up to authority.
Also called **kissing the boss's arse**, **sucking-up** or **crawling**.

budgie smugglers Men's swimmers
Also **dick pointers** and **Speedos**

bugger A great Aussie word with multiple uses:
bugger it! - annoyance.
bugger me! - surprise.
bugger off! - get lost!
buggerising around - wasting time.
buggered if I know - ignorance.
bugger (something) up - spoil, ruin.
bugger-all - nothing.
buggered - exhausted.

bull's roar A rough measure of distance - 'the place was so crowded we couldn't get within a bull's roar.'

bullshit Gross exaggeration and make-believe mixed with vivid imagination and a few lies. Thus 'bullshit artist' - one who flirts with the truth. As in politician.

bum steer To mislead someone - 'I gave him a bum steer.'

bum's rush Abrupt dismissal or rejection - 'when he asked for a raise, he was given the bum's rush'.

bunch of fives A clenched fist - 'If he doesn't shut up, I'll give him a bunch of fives.' An alternative is a **knuckle sandwich**.

bundle To 'drop one's bundle' - to give up and surrender all responsibility.

burn To 'go for a burn' is to go for a fast and sometimes dangerous car ride.

bush A general term for anywhere outside of the cities - 'he's gone bush.'
In a four-wheel drive on bush trails, it's called **bush-bashing**.

bushed One can be totally bushed (lost) or totally bushed (exhausted).

BYOG (BYO) Bring your own grog (booze)
A sign seen in unlicensed restaurants.

cactus Stuffed, rooted - 'I'm really cactus!'

cark it To die - old Charlie carked it, he's cactus, he fell off the perch, or he kicked the bucket.

chalkie Schoolteacher

chat To talk to someone. When a man '**chats-up**' a woman it is usually done with the intention of 'racing her off' for sexual purposes.

cheap shot A sneaky blow carried out when the recipient is not expecting it and has little chance to retaliate.

chip-in To donate money to assist someone else's cause - 'we'd better all chip-in for poor old Fred.' Also known as a 'whip-around.'

chock-a-block Full - 'the place was chock-a-block' or 'chockers.'
Sometimes 'chock-a-block up her' meaning a considerable degree of sexual success.

choof-off To leave - 'I think I'll choof off now.'
Polite for piss off.

chooks Barnyard fowls. The prize in the many 'chook raffles' held in Aussie pubs and clubs.

Christmas hold A rugby term describing a particularly nasty tackle where the tackler also grabs a handful of nuts. Exponents of this tackling style are known as **bag-snatchers**.

chrome-dome A bald-headed man

chop 'Get in for your chop' - grab your fair share.
'Not much chop' - something of doubtful value.
'Get the chop' - get fired.

chops Jaw - 'I gave him a smack in the chops.'

choppers Teeth
If false, they're called **clackers**.

chuck To throw - 'I chucked a stone at him.'
To vomit - 'I just had a chuck.'

clanger A bad mistake which one 'drops.'
'During his speech, he dropped a real clanger.'

claytons Any imitation or substitute.
From *Claytons Tonic*, an alcohol substitute.

clink Prison - 'they threw him in the clink.'
Many prefer to be in the '**slammer**.'

clobber Clothes - 'put on your good clobber.'
To bash someone - 'I'm going to clobber him!'

clue Vague, slow or just dumb people
'haven't got a clue' or are 'clueless.'
Bright people are 'very cluey.'

cocky A farmer
- cow cocky, wheat cocky, cane cocky etc.

coconut A Pacific Islander
Smarter to address them as 'sir.'

coldie A cold beer - can, bottle or draught.

come-good A reversal of otherwise poor form or
conditions - 'things should come-good soon.'

cop shop Police station

crack hardy To put on a brave front despite adversity - 'he's cracking hardy at the moment.'

crack it To achieve sexual success

cracker 'Not worth a cracker' - worth very little.

crafty A quick drink or two - 'let's nip down to the pub for a crafty.'

crash-hot An outstanding result. Sometimes '**shit-hot**' which means the same but more colourful.

crawl To suck-up to authority - 'he's a real crawler.'

cricket score A high score for all sports except cricket.

crook Unwell - 'jeeze I'm feeling crook.' To berate someone - 'I'll go crook at him when I see him.'

crumpet A bit of crumpet is either sexual success - 'I got a bit of crumpet' or an attractive woman who may be seen as 'not a bad bit of crumpet.'

crust Livelihood - 'what do you do for a crust?'

cunt The lexicographers of Aussie slang were pre-occupied with body parts, particularly the vital boy and girl bits. Cunt is certainly the nastiest word in the slang vocabulary and is mostly used between males as the ultimate Aussie insult - 'he's a cunt!'

Some softer options for the female nether region:

All quiet on the western front (all quiet)
Ballina Punt (Ballina)
box
Also the name of the protector used by cricketers to guard their sensitive bits.
bearded clam
beaver
drop kick and punt (drop kick)
fanny
freckle
gash
Thus **gash magnet**
- a bloke who's irresistible to women.
hairy cheque book
Some women pay by it.
map of Tasmania
The pubic area bears a close resemblance to the shape of Tasmania.
muff
Thus the term muff-diver.
nasty
pussy
Rex Hunt (Rex)
Australian TV personality.
snatch
wendy
Reference to the 'W' shape it makes in a girls pants - 'check out her wendy!'

daggy Someone or something which is unfashionable or grubby - 'he's a real dag.'

dead-set Real, true - 'he's a dead-set champion.'

deck To punch someone's lights out or 'deck' him - 'I had a fight with Harry last night and I decked him.'

dick-head A fool - 'he's a real dick-head.'
Some prefer the older term dill or the more modern words, dingaling and goose.
These are relatively mild terms of abuse. For those seriously into name-calling, these may satisfy: (in descending order of dislike)

ratbag
fuckwit
mongrel
bastard
rotten bastard
prick
shit
dead shit
turd
arsehole
cunt
dead cunt

digger Australian soldiers from WW1. Also a term of address among men - 'owyagoin digger,' (mate), (cobber)

dingo's breakfast
Very modest fare
- a drink of water and a good look around.

dip-out To withdraw from or lose out
- 'I dipped-out on the job.'

dish-lickers Greyhound racing dogs

dob-in To inform on someone
- 'I'll dob you in to the boss.'

dole bludger Someone on unemployment benefits who is not exactly rushing to join the ranks of the employed.

dog's disease
Influenza - 'I've got the dog's disease.'

doggy bag Provided by restaurateurs for uneaten food. Rarely given to the dog.

doggy-style Sex on all fours. Useful when watching TV.

donkey's years
A long time
- 'I haven't seen him for donkey's years.'

down under A foreigner's description of Australia

drum Describes the inside information on the prospects of a horse in a certain race
- 'I got the drum on this horse in the first.'
When the horse in question runs last - it 'didn't run a drum.'

dud Something worthless or counterfeit is a dud. You can be a **dud bash** - not good in bed or be **dudded** - cheated.

duds / dacks
A bloke's duds are his pants.
A woman's duds are something that blokes want to get into.

dunny A great Aussie word for the lavatory. Usually the free-standing variety in the backyard. Also 'shouse' (shithouse) or bog.

earbasher One who likes a chat and only stops talking to draw breath. Known to talk under water, under wet cement, or with a mouth full of marbles.

early-opener A pub which opens earlier in the morning than most and whose patrons - looking for a heart-starter - believe that whatever time it opens is not early enough.

emma chisit? Aussie for asking the price - 'how much is it?'

F...

fair dinkum True, genuine - 'are you fair dinkum?' Very real - 'he's a dinki-di Aussie' or he's 'dinkum.'

fair go A reasonable (sometimes unreasonable) chance to achieve one's goals. Everybody wants a fair go.

fang-farrier Dentist. As a matter of interest, a plumber is called a shit-strangler.

fart-arse To waste time with useless activity - 'he was fart arsing around.'

fat An erection

filthy To be very unhappy with someone - 'I was filthy on him.'

fires blanks An impotent man

flash Someone or something which is a bit showy or ostentatious. Conversely, 'not too flash' means a bit below average.

flip Someone just short of being a boofhead - 'he's a flip.'

flash it To offer others a quick peep at one's sexual organ.

flasher Someone who likes to expose himself to unsuspecting victims.

flat out /chat Very busy - 'I can't come today, I'm flat out.'

flick One can give another the flick (leave them) or get the flick (the sack).

floater A turd left somewhat inconsiderately in a swimming pool.

flog To flog something is to sell it - often under dubious circumstances.
Or flog the dog - masturbate.

fluff A fart. 'Who did a fluffer?' or 'who let Fluffy off the chain?'

foggiest To not have a clue
- 'I haven't got the foggiest notion.'

freight Money - 'did you bring the freight?'

front-up To make an appearance somewhere, particularly before a judge or magistrate
- 'I've got to front-up to the beak.'

fuck Has many uses apart from the basic use.
fuck about - waste time.
fuck me gently! - surprise.
fuck off! - get lost! go away!
fuck you! - dismissal, contempt.
fuck-all - nothing - 'he knows fuck all.'
fucked - exhausted.
fucked if I know - ignorance.
fuck-truck - shaggin wagon.
fucked-up - a total mess.
fuckwit - a stupid person.

fucking Not surprisingly, the subject of men 'having their way' is the most popular one for the architects of Aussie slang.
Some options:
any/some/a bit
'Are you getting any?'
banging/bonking
burying the bishop
doing jiggy-jiggy
doona dancing
getting a bit of crumpet
getting your oats
getting a knock
getting the end in
giving the ferret a run
going off
having a grunt/jump/polish
hiding the sausage
in the saddle
naughty
nookie
on the job
parking the prawn
poking
porking
punching the whiskers
quickie
root or a Wellington (boot)
ripping one off
screwing
shagging
slammin' the lamb
slipping a length
spearing the bearded clam
throwing a leg
Those who shag are called shaggers.
On completion, they are often tired (shagged) and suffer backache (shagger's back), particularly if doing it in a shaggin wagon.

full-bore The maximum - 'he was going full-bore.'

full-quid Bright, alert and in complete control - 'he's the full-quid.' Mostly used however in the negative - 'he's not the full-quid.'

funny-farm A mental asylum.
Sometimes **rat house** or **looney-bin**.

G...

galah An uncomplimentary term for another
An Australian native bird.

gang bang Group sex involving one woman and at least three or more men. The contest therefore becoming more or less equal.

gangbusters Usually a highly successful work project - 'we're going gangbusters.'

get set To get a bet in place

get stuffed! A serious rejection

goal To 'kick a goal' is to achieve success - 'he really kicked a goal.'

goer A hard-working, fast and efficient performer - 'he's a real goer.'

golly A large ball of phlegm

gone bung Broken or unworkable
-'the bloody thing's gone bung.'

gong An award
-'he got a gong for his community service.'
Worn out, tired
- 'I've had the gong, sword or dick.'

goodonya Aussie for 'good on you.' Americans say 'have a nice day.' Aussies say 'onya'

good sort An attractive young woman

go-off To achieve sexual objectives
- girls who 'go-off' are more sought after than those who don't.
For something to be stolen
- 'don't leave that around, it'll go-off.'
To putrefy - 'the milk's gone-off.'

goose An uncomplimentary term for another
- 'he's a real goose.'
You don't need a long neck to be a goose.

greasy spoon A cheap restaurant
Also called the '**chew and spew**.'

grope A man's clumsy attempt at sexual foreplay

grouse Excellent - 'extra grouse' is even better.

grouter To 'come the grouter' is to act in a way which is opportunistic and usually unfair to others.
From the Aussie two-up game.

gutfull Enough - 'I've had a gutfull of him.'

guts The stomach area - 'I hit him in the guts.'

gutser To 'come a gutser' is literally to fall over or figuratively to suffer a misfortune
- 'I came a gutser on that deal.'

guzzle To drink booze in excess.

handbrake The wife

hard word A serious sexual suggestion - 'he put the hard word on her.'

heart-starter The first drink of the day. Considered necessary by serious drinkers as a means of getting back to where they were the night before.

hip pocket nerve To hit someone where it really hurts - in the wallet.

holding 'How are you holding?' - how much money have you got left and perhaps I can borrow some?

hollow legs Said of one who can consume copious quantities of beer.

holy shit! Exclamation of surprise.

hoop Jockey

hughie Euphemism for God
When it starts to rain in the outback, farmers look to the sky and say 'send 'er down hughie!'

jack	A multi-purpose word: Hopefully you won't 'get the jack' - VD. You may 'get jack of someone' - tire of them. You may 'jack up' - refuse to do something. You may 'jack-off' - masturbate.
jackaroo	A young male trainee farm worker. The female counterpart is jillaroo.
jake	'She'll be jake' - everything will be OK.
jeeze	Exclamation of surprise, admiration or dismay - 'jeeze I'm feeling crook.' *Euphemism for Jesus.*
joker	A friendly term for a man - 'I haven't seen that old joker for years.'
jungle juice	Home-made booze

kick Hip pocket or wallet - 'how much have you got in your kick?' The 'cunning-kick' is a man's secret cache, hopefully unknown to his wife.

kick-on To stay late - usually at a party.

kick the bucket To die

king brown A large beer bottle
From the Australian king brown snake.

king-hit A big, surprise punch - 'she king-hit him.' Sometimes called a **knuckle sandwich**.

king-pin The leading social or workplace figure - 'he's the king-pin.'

knackered Tired and worn out - 'I'm feeling knackered.'

knackers Testicles, balls, nuts

knee-trembler
Sex in the standing position. Usually done between dances at the ball and not recommended for the over 40's.

knock To 'knock' someone is to disparage them. To **'get a knock'** is to get lucky sexually.

For a woman to be **'knocked up'** means that she's pregnant, 'up the duff,' or 'in the pudding club.' For a man, the term simply implies exhaustion.

To get a **'knock back'** is to be refused something - usually relates to sexual advances.

To get a **'knockdown'** to someone is to be introduced to them.

'On the knocker' means being very much on time.

knock on - to fumble the ball in rugby.

knockabout - a working class person.

A **'knock shop'** is a brothel.

knuckle sandwich A punch in the mouth
One who is skilled at this pastime is said to be able to 'go the knuckle.'

lair A dandy, who is perceived to be showy and ostentatious. Often '**mug lair**.'

larrikin A young street rowdie or someone who is just a little naughty
- 'he's not a bad bloke, but a bit of a larrikin.'

lash To make an attempt - 'I'll have a lash at it.'

laughing gear
Mouth - 'get your laughing gear around this.'

leg-opener Strong alcohol
Seen by opportunistic men as making women more sexually attainable.

legless Drunk - 'he was legless.'

liquid lunch Beer instead of food

living daylights
A serious degree of fright - 'he scared the living daylights (shit) out of me.'

lob To arrive. Usually at a party or social event - 'what time should we lob?'

lousy Usually means tightfisted or mean but can also describe someone with body lice.

love-glove A condom
Alternatives are:
banana bandana
dong-sarong
jump suit
probe-robe
raincoat
rascal-wrapper

lumbered To be arrested - 'I got lumbered last night.'

lunatic soup A general term for most booze

lunch The bulge in a man's groin area - 'check out his lunch!'

lung-buster Cigarette. Also **cancer sticks** and **coffin nails**.

lurk A dubious or very doubtful scheme - 'I got on to a good lurk.'

man hole cover A tampon

mangrove A promiscuous person.
An indiscriminate rooter.

map of Tasmania
A woman's pubic area.
The outline of Tasmania bears a remarkable likeness to that particular part.

mate A greeting which Aussie men give to just about anyone despite the fact that no real evidence of mateship exists.
Also useful because Aussies aren't good at remembering names.
Can be friendly -'gidday mate' or threatening -'listen mate!'

mate's rates A special price for those close to us.

matinee Sex in the afternoon - usually extra-marital.

meat market A bar or nightclub where amateur sex is readily available.

mile-high club
Membership requirement is to have actually done it in an aeroplane - preferably whilst flying. Even better if you're at 5,280ft.

missus The wife. Alternatives are:
The dragon
The handbrake
The leader of the opposition
She who must be obeyed
The war office

moniker Signature - 'put your moniker on this.'

mooning Bum baring or '**brown eye**.'

morning glory
An erection. Many erections seem to occur in the early hours, but most are false and proceed no further - called a piss-horn.
Also, sex in the morning.

motser A large amount of money
- 'he won a motser at the races.'

mug An uncomplimentary description of another - 'you're a mug!'

mulga Another word for the bush, outback or scrub

mungo A devotee of rugby league football. The rugby union equivalent is 'rah rah.'

nag Racehorse

Neville Nobody (Neville) A very low-profile person.

nick

'Nick off!' - get lost!

'Get nicked!' - much the same but stronger.

'I got nicked' - the wallopers (police) finally caught up with me.

'In good nick' - usually a car or person that is in good condition and well maintained.

'In the nick' - in jail.

'In the nick of time' - just in time.

no-hoper Someone with little to recommend him - 'he's a real no-hoper,' or a real 'nong.'

nookie A polite word for a fuck

nosh Food - 'let's have some nosh' or 'let's have a nosh-up'.

nutcracker A woman with large strong thighs. You'll have to figure it out.

nooner Sex for lunch

palate cleanser
An extra beer drunk after food and wine as a means of 'cleansing the palate.' Usually just called a 'cleanser.'

panic merchant
One who is easily given to panic

perve — To examine closely someone of the opposite (or same) sex - 'he was perving on her, she on him, he on him, or she on her.'

pig's arse! — A strong expression of disagreement

piker — One whose spirit is weak
- 'don't be a piker, go for it!'

pinch — To steal - 'he pinched the bloody thing!'

piss — The most popular term for urinating.
Men usually:
check the plumbing
damage the Doulton
drain the dragon
drain the main drain
empty the anaconda
have a hi-diddle-diddle (piddle)
have a hit and miss
have a Nelson (Nelson Riddle - piddle)
have a snakes (snakes hiss - piss)

have a splash/slash
have a spray
have a squirt
have a werris (Werris Creek - leak)
have a you and me (pee)
point percy at the porcelain
rinse the prince
shake hands with the unemployed
shake hands with the wife's best friend
shake the snake
siphon the python
splash the boots
take a leak
water the horse

Women prefer to:
go for a twinkle
powder the nose
spend a penny
split the rug

piss Apart from relieving oneself, there's:
all piss and wind - a boastful person.
piece of piss - easy.
piss horn - a false erection.
piss-up - a big drink.
piss off! (sorf) - go away!
pisspot - a drunk.
pissing into the wind - a futile effort.
pissed-off - being very annoyed.
pissing down - raining hard.
piss-poor/weak - a very weak effort.
weak as piss - lacking in character.

pissed Drunk
The most widely used word to describe the state of inebriation. Other options:

Adrian Quist (Adrian)
blind drunk (blind)
drunk as a skunk
elephant's trunk (drunk)
full as a boot
full as a fart
full as a state school
hammered
hosed
legless
Molly the monk (drunk)
molo
Mozart and Liszt
off your face
Roy Bull (full)
Schindler's List
shickered
shit-faced
sloshed
smashed
spastic
tanked
talking shorthand
'tired and emotional.'
wasted

plonk Wine as described by non-wine drinkers

pocket billiards
A man playing pocket billiards is covertly playing with himself.

poets' day Friday. Piss Off Early Tomorrow's Saturday

polish Fellatio - 'she gave me a polish.'

pole vaulting The way a man imagines he moves around when he has an erection.

poofter Homosexual. The most common word used by heterosexual males to describe homosexuals. Other more creative options are:
back door bandit
bats for the other side
chutney-packer
Doris Day (gay)
freckle-puncher
fruit (cake)
horse's hoof
mattress-muncher
pillow-biter
pork and bean (queen)
queer
rear gunner/admiral
ring-jockey
shirt-lifter
toe-toucher
turd-burglar
Vegemite-driller
woolly woofter

pommy All Englishmen

posted To be stood up - 'she left me posted.'

prang A usually not-too-serious car crash.
Sometimes called a bingle.

prick Penis
Only doctors and mothers use the word penis.
Others choose from these:
beef bayonet
Boris Becker (pecker)
clam-digger
corned beef telescope
dick
donger
donk
doodle
eight day clock (cock)
ferret
John Thomas
lamb lance
mutton dagger
one-eyed trouser snake
pink cigar
pork sword
pyjama python
rascal
Rupert Murdoch (cock)
sex serpent
slug
snag
sperm worm
the middle stump
the old fella
tool
trouser snake
willie

prick-teaser A girl who leads a man on but has no intention of going all the way.

pub crawl The time-honoured Aussie custom of visiting as many pubs as possible in one serious drinking session.

puddin' club Pregnant - 'she's in the puddin' club.'

punt To gamble on the horses - thus the term 'punter.'

put in 'Put in the time' - do your fair share of work.
'Put someone in' - to inform on them.
'Who put in?' - the question asked when a quiet but deadly fart is in the air.

quack	The doctor (not always uncomplimentary)
quickie	A brief sexual encounter
quid	A pound before decimal currency

race-off To take someone away for the purpose of seduction. Done overtly by males and covertly by females.

rags Clothes. Also sanitary napkins.

ralph / ruth A vomit or chunder - 'where's Charlie? He's gone for a ralph.'

rack off! 'Get lost!'

ratshit Feeling crook - 'I was ratshit,' or 'I was R.S.'

rev-head A fast-driving car freak. Also 'petrol head.'

roadie A last drink for the road - sometimes the last drink ever!

room-clearer A particularly nasty fart

rooted Tired and exhausted - 'I'm feeling rooted.' Has only a remote connection with the aftermath of sexual intercourse.

rubbish To dismiss another's views - 'to rubbish someone.'

rug rat A small child

S...

salad dodger An overweight person

sandwich A tricky sexual arrangement between two men and a woman.
Can be done vertically or horizontally.

sanger Sandwich

schooner A 15oz (425 ml) glass of beer

scoot To depart - 'I'm going to scoot.'

scorcher A very hot day - 'It's a real scorcher.'

scrub The outback
- 'he comes from somewhere up the scrub.'
To cancel or discard
- 'the plan wasn't working so we scrubbed it.'

scrubber An uncomplimentary term used by males to describe certain females - 'she's a real scrubber.'

scrub-up To improve greatly one's appearance by dress and grooming - 'he scrubs up well.'

scumbag A rather uncomplimentary description of another - 'he's a real scumbag.' Given new life by ex-Prime Minister Keating.

scunge A badly groomed or badly behaved person - 'she's a real scunge.'

seagull A rugby term for a forward who avoids his centre-field responsibilities by lurking on the wing.

serve/spray To give someone a serve (spray) is to verbally harangue another - 'I gave him a real serve.'

shaft To shaft someone, is figuratively to stab them in the back - 'the bastard shafted me.'
Also a word for playing hide the sausage.

shickered Being shickered is not quite as serious as being pissed.

shemozzle A state of confusion. A real mess - 'the meeting was a real shemozzle'.
Or a shambles.

shit-kicker One who does manual labour or menial tasks

shit Has a wide variety of uses apart from defecation:
a lot of shit - nonsense
a real shit fight - an angry scene
a shit load - large quantity
happy as a pig in shit - very happy
he doesn't give a shit - indifferent
he scared the shit out of me - fear
he's a real (dead) shit! - contempt
he's a shit-kicker - insignificant
he's got shit for brains - stupid
holy shit! - surprise
in the shit - in trouble

in deep shit - in real trouble
not worth a pinch of shit - worthless
rat shit - feeling poorly
scarce as rocking horse shit
shit! or shit a brick! - angry exclamation
stiff shit! - bad luck!
shit on the liver - in a bad mood
shithead - an uncomplimentary term
for another
shit-faced - drunk
shithouse - dunny
shits are trumps - we have a big problem.
shit-scared- fear
shit-hot - a good result
to shit-in - to win comfortably
wouldn't give you the steam
off his shit - mean

shitters ditch

A WW1 term which described the trenches where soldiers lived and fought. Now used to describe one who is in very big trouble - 'he's really in shitters ditch.'

shonky Someone or something of doubtful integrity - 'he's very shonky and so is the deal.'

shoot through

To depart
Leisurely - 'I think I'll shoot through now.'
Hastily - 'we'd better shoot through.'

short-arse In newspeak, a vertically-challenged person.

shout To buy drinks in rounds
'Your shout' - your turn to buy the drinks.

shot 'That's the shot' - that's right or good.
To 'take a shot' at something is to give one's best effort.
To 'have a shot' at someone is to criticise them - 'he had a shot at me.'

shrapnel Loose change

sickie A day taken off work because of illness. Usually spent at the beach, on the golf course, at the cricket or in the pub.

silvertail A name given to the 'haves' by the 'have-nots.'

skid-marks Brown stains on underwear. At the front of the underwear, the marks are called snail-trails.

skinny dipping Nude bathing

skint Broke - 'I'm skint.'

skite A skiter is one who through boasting and bragging, becomes a pain in the arse.

slammer Prison. Where wallopers put you when you misbehave. Some prefer to be in the 'clink.'

sling A special payment, bribe or secret commission. Winning racehorse owners often 'sling' the jockey.

sling-off To deride or ridicule someone
- 'she was slinging-off at me.'

slog Hard work - 'that was a hard slog.'

slops Alcohol (usually beer)
- 'old Charlie's on the slops again.'

sloshed The result of being on the booze
- 'I got really sloshed last night.'

slug To overcharge
- 'they slug you at that place.'
Also slang for penis.

smart aleck/arse
A boastful person who thinks he knows a lot, but mostly knows bugger-all (nothing)
- 'he's a real smart arse.'

sparrow's fart
Early morning
- 'I'll pick you up at sparrow's.'

spew Vomit
A bodily function which receives a lot of attention from the slang-makers.

Options are:
calling for B.e.r.t, G.e.o.r.g.e or R.u.t.h
driving the porcelain bus
going the big spit
having a chuck
having a chunder or 'up and under'
having a liquid laugh

laughing at the lawn
on the big white telephone
technicolour yawn

Curiously, the contents of a technicolour yawn always contain fragments of carrots despite the fact that none have recently been eaten.

spit chips To suffer from anger and frustration - 'the boss was spitting chips.'

spot-on Absolutely right, accurate - 'the report was spot-on.'

squib A coward - 'he squibbed it.'

squirt Has a number of uses:
'He's just a squirt' - a small child.
'Just a squirt thanks' - only a small drink.
'To get on the squirt' - serious drinking.
'To go for a squirt' - taking a leak.

starkers Naked - 'she was completely starkers.'
Other options used when naked and nude were naughty words:
in the altogether
in the bollocky
in the buff
in the nuddy
in the raw

stickybeak An overly inquisitive person

stiff To be stiff is to be very unlucky - 'he was real stiff.'
May also apply to a man who is about to get lucky sexually or is dead.

stiff-shit! Said sarcastically to one who complains about his general misfortune.

stiffy An erection - 'I have a stiffy.'
Also, woody, fat or horn.

stony-broke Being very short of funds - 'I'm stony-broke.'

stoush A pub or street fight - 'I got into a stoush last night.'

stroppy Someone who is angry, difficult or has a bad case of the tom-tits.

stubbie A small beer bottle

stuffed Exhausted - 'I'm totally stuffed.'
More polite than being shagged, buggered, knackered, rooted or just plain fucked.
All terms have obvious sexual links.

'straya' Australia
Sadly, few Aussies can correctly pronounce the name of their country.

suss To determine all the possibilities of a situation - 'let's suss out all the options.'
Also suspicious - 'that deal was a bit suss.'

swan around
To be looking good but actually doing bugger-all

sword swallower
A lady who enjoys variation in her sex life

talent Desirable members of both sexes - 'let's go to the beach and check out the talent.'

tall poppies Successful people whom the unsuccessful want to cut down to their size.

tan track The anus

tanked Drunk

tart A woman with a dubious sexual reputation

tinnie A can of beer or a small aluminium boat

town To 'go to town' on something is to get stuck into it - to give it your best.

traps To 'go around the traps' is to check one's regular haunts.

trot When things are going well - you're having a **good trot**. When things are going badly - you're having a **bad trot**.

trots Severe diarrhoea - 'I've got the trots.' Also harness racing.

tube A can of beer

turd A shit.

turd strangler
A plumber

turps Alcohol, booze - 'he's on the turps again.'

tyke Roman Catholic. Also left-footer, mick, kneeler, cattle ticks.

waccy baccy Marijuana

walloper A policeman. Usually spoken about them rather than to them.

wank Male masturbation.
Alternatives are:
beat the meat
burping the worm
flog the dog/log/lizard
have a pull/flip/toss
jerk/jack off
jerkin' the gherkin
pound the pork
pull the pud
spank the monkey
wank the plank

wanker Someone who is odd, eccentric, lives in another world, masturbates regularly or is just plain objectionable.

wedge An extra drink which serious drinkers have if the rest of the group is a bit slow.
A 'tweenie' in Sydney's eastern suburbs.

whinger One who is always complaining
- 'he's a bloody whinger.'

whippy A pool of money contributed to by a group. There can also be a 'secret whippy' or cache which a man often has to keep his wife from getting.

whizz off To depart - 'I think I'll whizz off now.'

wobbly An outburst of anger
One 'throws' or 'chucks' a wobbly.
Much the same as spitting the dummy.

wobbly boots
Said of one who is pissed
- 'he's wearing his wobbly boots.'

wombat A sexually promiscuous man. He eats, roots, shoots and leaves.

wood To 'have the wood on someone' is to know their weaknesses.

woofy Smelly - 'he's a bit woofy under the Warwicks.'
'Warwicks' is short for 'Warwick Farms,' rhyming slang for arms.

wrap/rap To lavish praise - 'I gave him a big wrap.'

yack — To have a yack is to have a chat

yakka — Work - 'that was hard yakka.'

y-fronts — Blokes' undies

yips — Fear and anxiety leading to reduced performance
- 'he had the yips and missed a one foot putt.'
Sometimes called the heeby-jeebies.

yonks — A long time - 'I haven't seen him for yonks.'

yobbo — The uncouth Aussie male noted for bad behaviour, particularly at sporting events.
Alternatives are ocker or yahoo.
The female counterpart is 'shirl.'

GREAT Aussie Phrases

"If your auntie
had balls,
she'd be your uncle!"

a bit of all right

Usually a man's description of a good looking woman - 'she's a bit of all right' or 'she's a good sort.'

a bit of arse/crumpet/skirt

A woman as a sex object.

all over red rover

All done, all finished, end of section.

all piss and wind

A boastful and insincere person - 'he's all piss and wind.'

all your Christmases/birthdays have come at once

When very good fortune comes your way.

any tick of the clock

Any moment now.

argue the toss

To argue against the odds or to just argue.

around the twist/bend

Crazy - 'If I don't get out of here soon, I'll go round the twist.'

arse-about-face

A total reversal or back-to-front - 'he's got it all arse-about.'

arse beats class

When good luck wins out over good reputation. A variation is 'bullshit baffles brains.'

arse out of his pants

Someone who is down and out.

arse over tit

To fall heavily or be knocked down
- 'I knocked him arse over tit.'
The polite form is 'base over apex' or 'A over T.'

avagoodweegend!

What Aussie workmates say to each other on Friday afternoon. Also **'javagoodweegend?'** which is said by the same people on Monday morning.

away with the pixies/fairies

One who is totally out of touch with reality
- 'he's away with the pixies.'

bag your head!
bight your bum!
get stuffed!/fucked!/rooted!
in your boot!
pull your head in!
stick it up your arse/jumper!
up yours for the rent!

Said when your usual powers of diplomacy fail you.

bats and bowls

A bi-sexual.

belt the living daylights

To give someone a beating - 'I belted the living daylights out of him.'

better than a poke in the eye with a sharp stick

A poor, but under the circumstances, preferable alternative.

bite the bullet

To face up to an unavoidable or unpleasant task.

bore it up em!

A sporting term meaning to strongly press home the team's decided advantage.

boy/man in the boat

Clitoris.

break it down!

An exclamation demanding of fair play.

bright-eyed and bushy-tailed

Someone full of health and vigour and raring to go.

Buckley's chance

A very forlorn chance, or no hope.
'You've got two chances - yours and Buckley's.'
Derived from Melbourne store Buckley and Nunn.

bullshit baffles brains

Slick talk often wins over superior knowledge.

bumping uglies

Fucking.
With lesbians it's called bumping bonnets.

bun in the oven

Pregnant or 'up the duff.'

bung it on

To put on affectation or 'side.'

bung on a blue

To start a fight.

butter wouldn't melt in his mouth

A person of angelic, but deceptive appearance.

by the length of the straight

A clear winner. 'Daylight second' is another option.

can't take a trick

Nothing going right - 'I can't take a trick today.'

carries on like a pork chop

Irrational behaviour.

caught short

To have an urgent need to choke a darkie.

choke/strangle a darkie

To defecate. People talk about 'taking' a shit when actually they 'leave it.'

come off it!

A statement of cynical disbelief.

cop a dose

Gaining very unwelcome side-effects
from getting your end in.

cop it sweet

To take your punishment manfully.
To accept admonishment without complaint.

crack a fat/horn

Achieving an erection.

crack hardy

Putting on a brave front despite serious problems.

cruel someone's pitch

Spoiling another's plans - 'he's doing well with that sheila but I'll try to cruel his pitch.'

cut some slack

To give someone room to move - 'I'll cut him some slack.'

damage the Doulton

To use the lavatory.

daylight second

Describes a very clear winner - 'when he won, it was daylight second.'

didn't come down in the last shower

Someone who is no fool and not easily led.

didn't run a drum

Usually describes a poorly-performed horse.

dining at the Y
munching on the muffin
muff diving
going down

A very popular male sexual pastime.
You'll have to figure it out.

do a runner/flit

To do a fast exit from a restaurant before the Jack and Jill (bill) arrives.

do the trick

To achieve the desired result - 'that'll do the trick.'

do your block/nana

To lose your temper.

doesn't know if he's Arthur or Martha
doesn't know if he's bored or punched

Someone in a total state of confusion.

don't come the raw prawn!

Don't give me that bullshit!

don't get your knickers in a knot!
don't get your bowels in a twist!
don't get your tits in a tangle!

Don't get upset - just relax.

don't give a rat's arse!

Total indifference.

down in the dumps

Depressed, gloomy, sad
- 'I'm feeling down in the dumps.'

down the gurgler/drain
A plug hole where one's gambling winnings often finish up.

down the hatch!
Popular Aussie drinking toast.

dragging the chain
Not keeping up with everybody else in a drinking session.

drink with the flies
One who chooses to, or is forced to drink alone.

drop your bundle
To lose control - 'he dropped his bundle.'

drown some worms
Fishing.

fair crack of the whip
fair suck of the sav (saveloy)
A demand for fair play - 'be reasonable, do it my way.'

fell off the back of a truck
Something stolen or of questionable origin.

first cab off the rank
To be the first to take advantage of an opportunity.

from arsehole to breakfast time
Covered all over
- 'he was mud from arsehole to breakfast time.'

full of shit
Someone who is given to boasting - 'he's full of shit.'

get a load

To acquire an unwanted rash (or worse) from a bit of stray poking.
Also 'get a load of that!' - take a look at that!

get in for your chop

To push ahead for your share of whatever it is that's going.

get-it-interya

A pub term for 'drink up.'

get stuck into it

To tackle enthusiastically the task at hand.
To get stuck into someone is to fight them.

get the bullet

To be relieved of one's employment or 'let go.'
Alternatives are:
get the flick or be flicked
get the arse
get the chop
get the hammer - hammer and tack, RS for sack.
get the pink slip
get the shove
get the DCM (don't come Monday)

get your arse into gear

Get ready - be prepared to do some work.

getting your arse in a sling

Getting into big trouble.

getting your end in

Men come from a certain place and spend the rest of their lives trying to get back there.
Also referred to as 'getting a bit,'
or for a married man, 'getting a bit on the side.'

getting off at Redfern
Coitus interruptus.
Redfern is just one train station before Central.

give it a bash/burl/lash
To make an attempt - 'I'll give it a bash.'

give it the herbs
To rapidly accelerate a car.

give the ferret a run
Sexual intercourse - 'I'll give the ferret a run tonight.'

go for a row
To receive severe punishment for wrongdoing.
'The wallopers caught him and it looks like he'll go for a row.'

go for the doctor
To go all the way - to do one's best.

go for your life
Curiously this means 'go right ahead, be my guest.'

go the knuckle
One who is very capable in a fist fight -'he can really go the knuckle.'

gone bananas
Someone who is very agitated or has lost control.

gone a million
You have only a very slim chance or no chance of achieving your goal - 'you're gone a million.'

had the gong/sword/dick

Tired, beaten, can't go on - 'I've had the gong.'
Some prefer 'had the Richard' (dick) or 'had the sword.'

half a mongrel/brute/larrikin/bar

An oncoming erection.

have two bob each way

To be so undecided as to hedge the bet or
'sit on the fence.'

having it off

Sexual intercourse
- he's having it off - she's having it off.

hawk the fork

The commercial arrangement made by hookers.

head down, arse up

One who is very busy working
- 'I was head down, arse up all day.'

hide/sink the sausage
park the tiger/prawn
slip a length

Getting your end in.

hip pocket nerve

To hit where it hurts - in the wallet.

home and hosed

A racecourse certainty
- 'he's home and hosed' or 'home and dried.'
A horse which is seen as likely to be back in the stalls
while the other horses are still running.

hope your balls turn into bicycle wheels and back-pedal up your arse

hope your chooks turn into emus and kick your dunny down

Great Aussie curses.

horizontal folk dancing

Sexual intercourse.

horses for courses

The selection of the appropriate person for a particular task.

hot to trot

Eager and willing to commence - 'he's hot to trot.'

if your auntie had balls, she'd be your uncle!

The answer to someone who persists in complaining about what could have happened - if only......

in more shit than a Werribee duck

in the shit/poo

In big trouble.

in the family way

Pregnant.
Some prefer 'up the duff.'

in the saddle

'On the job' - doing a bit of poking.

in your face

Aggressive and intimidating behaviour.
Mostly associated with today's 'sportsmen.'

is the Pope a Catholic?
does Rose Kennedy have a black dress?
do bears shit in the woods?

Stock answers to a question for which the answer is clearly yes.

keeping one for Ron

When offered one item, take two and keep one for Ron (later on).

kick a goal

To achieve considerable success
- 'when he got that new job he really kicked a goal.'

kick the tin

To contribute to a collection box or tin.

living on the smell of an oily rag

One who manages to live on very little.

long streak of pelican shit
if he turns sideways he's marked absent

A tall thin person.

more arse than Jessie
more arse than class

Success through good luck rather than good management.

more...than you can poke a stick at

More than enough.

most fun you can have with your clothes on

The second best feeling you know.

mushroom treatment

Keeping someone in the dark and feeding them bullshit.

necking it

Drinking wine from the bottle.

no flies on him

A very smart person.

no room to swing a cat

Very little space.

not much chop

Not very good.

not worth a cracker/sausage/crumpet

Worthless.

not worth a cunt full of cold water

not worth a pinch of shit

Less than worthless.

off with the pixies

A vague and absent-minded person.

off your face

Drunk - 'he's off his face.'

on a promise

To be promised sexual favours
- 'I'm on a promise tonight.'

on the ball

One who is alert and very aware of what's happening
- 'he's on the ball.'

on the big white telephone
driving the porcelain bus

Having a chunder or technicolour yawn into the toilet bowl.

on the blink

Something that is not working - 'the beer's warm because the bloody fridge is on the blink.'
Alternatives are:
gone bung
conked out
had the sword
had the dick
stuffed
rooted
fucked
completely fucked
On the blink usually applies to machinery. The alternatives can also apply to people.

More 'on' phrases:

on a promise - a promise of sexual favours.
on the bight - looking for a loan.
on the blower - on the telephone.
on the dole - being paid to do bugger-all.
on the house - free.
on the job - having sex.
on the loose - free and available.
on the make - bent on sexual conquest.
on the nod - betting on credit.
on the nose/bugle - very smelly.
on the outer - unpopular.
on the piss/grog/squirt/sauce/slops - serious drinking.
on the punt - betting on horses.
on the ropes - in danger of failing.
on the run - a jump ahead of the law.
on the shelf - a seriously unmarried woman.
on the side - extra marital sex.
on the skids - going nowhere fast.
on the sly - secretive.
on the take - receiving illegal payments.
on the trot - a succession of wins.
on the vinegar stroke - the point of sexual climax.
on the (water) wagon - not drinking.

over the fence/odds

Unreasonable, unacceptable
- 'their offer was over the fence.'

packing the shits

Very scared
- 'things were so bad, I was packing the shits.'

pass in the marble
fall off the perch
put the cue in the rack
cark it

To die.

pass the buck
To unfairly place responsibility with someone else.

pay with the hairy cheque book
Sexual favours in lieu of payment.

pick the bones out of that one
A statement made by one who has just farted in company and feels the need to alert others of his action.

pick the eyes out of
To select the best of a number of options.

piss or get off the pot!
Do something now or get out of the way.

pissing in someone's pocket
Bestowing excessive and insincere flattery.

pissing into the wind
A futile attempt to do something with little or no chance of success.

pissing it up against the wall
Wasting money on booze - 'he made a heap, but pissed it all up against the wall.'

pissing razor-blades
Usually the painful result of indiscriminate sex.

play silly-buggers
To engage in time-wasting or frivolous activity.

plays piano in a brothel
Someone who is actually employed
but is not too fussy about how, where or by whom.

pull the plug/rug

To finally give up on a project
- 'we're going to pull the plug on that deal.'

pull up stumps

To end a project for the day or permanently.

punch the whiskers/pants

A man's somewhat indelicate description of getting his end in.

punch your lights out

Usually more a threat than a reality
- 'I wanted to punch his lights out.'

pushing shit uphill with a sharp stick

Someone bent on a hopeless mission or an enterprise doomed to failure.

put the bite on

To borrow or cadge money
- 'I'm a bit short this week, I'll put the bite on Charlie.'

put the cat among the pigeons

To create havoc and confusion.

put the cue in the rack

To retire gracefully or to die
- 'old George has put his cue in the rack.'
Also, to retire from sexual activity.

put the hard word/acid on

To make strong sexual overtures. Done by both sexes.

put the mockers on

To bring bad luck or to jinx a person or a project
- 'that bastard put the mockers on me.'

puts lead in your pencil

Certain food and drinks which are somewhat optimistically believed to increase male sexual performance.

rip one off

Blokes' talk for getting your end in.
Also means to let go a fart.

same horse, different jockey

A promiscuous or much-married woman.

scream blue murder
scream your tits off

To complain loudly.

she'll be right!

An expression of confidence and reassurance.

she's had more pricks than a second-hand dartboard

A woman with considerable sexual experience.

short arms and deep pockets
death adders/mousetraps in his pocket

Descriptions of the miserly.
Often those who avoid their shout at the bar.

shut the gate

A statement made when it appears that the winner is obvious - 'he's so far in front it's shut the gate.'

since Jesus played fullback for Jerusalem

A long time ago.

spit the dummy

A sudden display of anger and petulance causing what is known as a **'dummy spit.'**

split the rug

Girls' talk for taking a piss.

strike a blow

To go to work - 'let's strike a blow.'

suits me down to the ground

An ideal plan or result
- 'that suits me right down to the ground.'

swear on a stack of Bibles

To affirm with great sincerity
- 'I'll swear on a stack of Bibles.'

taking the mickey/piss

Using sarcasm to put someone down
- 'he took the piss out of me.'

the whole box and dice

Everything
- 'after the divorce, she got the whole box and dice.'

through to keeper

To ignore a remark
- 'we'll let that one go through to the keeper.'
Borrowed from cricket.

trap for young players

A hazard for the unwary.

two-bob each way

Hedging one's bet or **'sitting on the fence.'**

two-pot screamer

One who gets pissed very easily.

up a gum tree
up shit creek without a paddle

Someone in big trouble with few options available.

up the duff

Pregnant
she's up the duff
she's got a bun in the oven
she's in the pudding club

walk up start

A person or horse with a decided advantage in a particular contest.

we'll be there when the whips are cracking

We'll be on time for the main event.

went mad and they shot him

Whereabouts unknown.
'Where's Harry?' - 'he went mad and they shot him.'

wet enough to bog a duck

wet the whistle
splash the tonsils

To have a drink.

when the shit hits the fan

You're in big trouble.

where the crows fly backwards to keep the sun out of their eyes

A very remote outback place.

where the sun doesn't shine
where your mother never kissed you

Your bum

within spitting distance

Very close

won by the length of the straight

A clear winner.

would freeze the balls off a brass monkey

Description of a very cold day.

would kill a brown dog

Usually refers to lousy food.

would blow a dog off the chain

A very windy day.

wouldn't be dead for quids

An expression of wellbeing.
'I wouldn't be dead for quids' (old currency)
Also 'wouldn't miss it for quids.' A very important engagement.

wouldn't know him from a bar of soap
wouldn't know him from a bull's foot
wouldn't know him if he stood up in my porridge

Very much a stranger.

wouldn't touch it/him with a 40 foot pole

Something/someone who is to be carefully avoided.

your hook!

Your shout - it's your turn to buy a drink.

"You're lookin' happy John"
"Yeah - I'm gunna to give the ferret a run tonight"

Great Aussie people descriptions

A few ways that Aussies describe each other. They may sound a little severe but are essentially whimsical and usually good-natured.

he's...

a cabbage short of a coleslaw
a chop short of a barbecue
a few bricks short of a load
a sandwich short of a picnic
a stubbie short of a six-pack
a waste of space
got kangaroos in the top paddock
not playing with the full deck
missing a few spots on his dominoes
not the full quid/bottle
not the sharpest knife in the cutlery drawer
not the sharpest tool in the shed
one shingle short of a roof
two palings short of a fence

he hasn't got both paddles/oars in the water
the lift doesn't reach the top floor
there's a light on but nobody's at home

he's got a face...

like a bashed crab
like a busted bum (arsehole)
like the back end of a bus
like the dark side of the moon
like a dropped pie
like a foot
like a half chewed Mintie
like a Mallee root

he's got a head...

like a beaten favourite
like a robber's dog
like a twisted sandshoe
that would get him out of jury duty

he's got a mouth like a horse collar

Large and constantly moving.

he'd talk under water with a mouth full of marbles
he'd talk under wet cement
he'd talk you blind

Likes a chat

he'd give an Aspro a headache

he's got death adders/mousetraps in his pocket
he's got short arms and deep pockets

Not given to buying a drink when it's his turn.

he's got his head up his arse
he's got tickets on himself
he thinks his shit doesn't stink
he thinks the sun shines out of his arse
he's up himself

Conceited.

he's got more arse than Jessie

Usually means someone who enjoys a great deal of luck, but can be used to describe someone with a lot of hide (cheek)

Jessie was a famous Sydney Zoo elephant.

he's got more front than Myers

Hide, cheek, effrontery.

Myers is a large retail chain.

he's got more movements than a Swiss watch

A bit dodgy.

he's got a smile like a busted watermelon

Not pretty.

he's got rocks in his head
he's got shit for brains

Dumb.

he's got shit on the liver

In a bad mood.

he hasn't got a pot to piss in
he hasn't got a sausage/cracker

Has few assets.

he's hung like a Mallee bull

Has better than average-size genitals.

he's in more trouble than Speed Gordon

Has big troubles.

he couldn't...

blow the froth off a beer
carry a tune if it had a handle on it
catch a cold
fight his way out of a wet paper bag
find his arse in the dark with both hands
find the grand piano in a one-roomed house
give a flying fuck
give a rat's arse (indifference)
go two rounds with a revolving door
hit a bull in the bum with a handful of wheat
knock the dags off a sick canary
organise a fart in a baked bean factory
organise a fuck in a brothel with a handful of $50's
organise a piss-up in a brewery
organise a shit fight in a septic tank

pick a seat at the pictures
pull the skin off a rice pudding
run out of sight on a dark night
tell the time if the town hall clock fell on him
train a choko vine over a country dunny

he wouldn't...

have a clue
know if a tram was up him unless the conductor rang the bell
know if he had a bus up his bum unless someone got out
know his arse from his elbow
know if his arse was on fire
know if you were up him
know shit from clay
know which way was up
work in an iron lung

so mean he wouldn't...

give a rat a railway pie
give you a fright if he was a ghost
give you a light for your pipe at a bushfire
give you a shock if he owned the powerhouse
give you a wave if he owned the ocean
give you the sleeves out of his vest
give you the steam off his shit
give you the time of day
give you the wind off his fart
piss on you if you were on fire
shout if a shark bit him
he's still got his first zac (sixpence)
he's still got his lunch money from school

If you were having a Roman orgy, you'd send him out for the grapes

Not much use

so low...

he can parachute out of a snake's belly
he gets upgraded to economy class

so poor...

he hasn't got a pot to piss in
he'd lick the paint off the fence

so randy...

he'd root a fly on the wing
he'd root an old boot

so strong...

he'd hold a bull out to piss

so ugly...

he'd make a train take the dirt road

so hungry...

I could chew the crutch out of an
Afghan camel driver's jocks.
I could eat the crutch out of a low-flying duck
I could eat the crutch out of a rag doll
I could eat the horse and chase the rider
my stomach thinks my throat's cut

so thirsty...

I could drink through a dead dog's arsehole
I've got a thirst that would cast a shadow
I've got a thirst you could photograph

"Mate,
I've been flat out like
a lizard drinking"

AS...

(Some colourful **'as'** comparisons)

People descriptions:

He's as....

bald as a badger
blind as a bat
bold as brass (cheeky)
boring as bat shit
bright as a button (smart)
cool as a cucumber (relaxed)
crazy as a loon
crazy as a two-bob watch
cunning as a shithouse rat
deaf as a post
drunk as a skunk
fat as a pig
hard as nails (tough)
low as a shark's tit
low as a snake's belly
sharp as a tack (smart)
silly as a two-bob watch
skinny as a rake
solid as a rock (reliable)
thick as a brick (stupid)
thick as two planks (stupid)
tight as a fish's arse (miserly)
ugly as a box full of blowflies
ugly as a hatfull of arseholes
weak as piss
Australian as a meat pie
Australians are noted for their passion for meat pies.
black as the ace of spades
Usually refers to a description of the night, sometimes a person.

busy as...

busy as a one-armed billposter in a gale
busy as a one-armed brickie in Beirut
busy as a one-armed cab driver with the crabs
busy as a one-armed paper hanger
busy as a one-legged man in a bum-kicking contest
Situations requiring considerable effort under difficult circumstances.

camp as...

camp as a row of tents
camp as Chloe
Heterosexual's descriptions of homosexuals.

cheap as chips

Very inexpensive.

clean as a whistle

Clean, tidy, neat and efficient.

cold as...

cold as a fish
(lacking in human warmth and emotion)
cold as a frog
cold as a maggot
cold as a polar bear's bum

cold as a witch's tit
cold as a mother-in-law's kiss
cold as a nun's nasty
(low body temperature)

crook as...

crook as a dog
crook as Rookwood
Crook as in sick or feeling very unwell, often from a hangover.
Rookwood is a Sydney cemetery.

crooked as a dog's hind leg

A very dodgy character.

dead as...

dead as a dodo
dead as a doornail
dead as a maggot
A dodo is a clumsy, flightless and extinct bird.

dry as...

dry as a bone
dry as a chip
dry as a dead dingo's donger
dry as a Pommy's bath towel
Exclamations of the very thirsty.

drunk as a skunk

easy as...

easy as falling off a log
easy as shitting in bed
A very easy task.

fit as...

fit as a fiddle
fit as a flea
fit as a trout
fit as a Mallee bull
The Mallee is rough scrub country in Victoria where anything that lives has to be very fit.

flat as a tack...

Refers to one's wellbeing as well as topography - 'I'm as flat as a tack.'

full as...

full as an all-stations train
full as a boot
full as a bull's bum
full as a doctor's wallet
full as a fairy's phone book
full as a fart
full as a fat lady's socks
full as a goog (egg)
full as a tick
Can't eat or drink any more - 'I'm as full as a fart.'
full as a seaside shithouse on bank holiday
full as a State school (hat rack)
Crowded.

funny as a fart in a phone box

Certainly not very funny if you're in the phone box and the fart's not yours.

game as Ned Kelly

Notorious Australian bushranger who managed to achieve hero status despite being a serious law-breaker.

good as gold

A common response to the 'owya goin mate, orright?' question.

happy as...

happy as a lark
happy as Larry
Larry Foley was a tough street fighter from Sydney's Rocks area around 1870. Also known as Larry Dooley, thus the description of a serious fight. Apparently Foley enjoyed his work.
happy as a pig in mud/shit
happy as a possum up a gum tree
Degrees of happiness.

lucky as a bastard on Father's Day

Unlucky.

mad as...

mad as a cut snake
mad as a gum tree full of galahs
mad as a hatter *(Australian bushman)*
mad as a meat axe
Mad (insane) rather than mad (angry).

nervous as a long-tailed cat in a room full of rocking chairs

phoney as a three dollar bill

Somebody or something which is very dubious.

pissed as a fart
pissed as a newt
high as a kite

Seriously drunk.

poor as a bandicoot

Of wretched character.

poor as a church mouse

Of very limited means.

popular as a bag full of fleas
popular as a pork chop in a synagogue
popular as a brown snake in a sleeping bag

Very unpopular.

randy as a mallee bull
randy as a snake

Excessive sexual energy.

rare as rocking-horse shit
scarce as hen's teeth

Commodities in short supply.

rough as bags/guts

One who is coarse, ill-mannered and considerably lacking in style.

sick as a dog
slow as a wet week in a caravan
small as gnats' nuts
small as a mozzie's cossie

smooth/bare as a baby's bum
stiff as an undertaker

Unlucky.

sweet as a nut

Don't worry, everything's in order - 'she's sweet.'

tight as a fish's arse – watertight

Describes one who is mean or has short arms and deep pockets.

tight as a mouse's ear

Describes the vital part of a sexually inexperienced young lady.

toey as ten men

Someone who is anxious for action - often sexual.

useful as...

useful as an ashtray on a motorbike
useful as a hip pocket on a singlet
useful as a glass door on a dunny

useless as...

useless as a bull's tit
useless as a chocolate teapot
useless as a handbrake on a Holden
useless as the Pope's balls
Also useless.

weak as piss

Someone lacking in character and moral resolution.

"I've got a
thirst that'd cast
a shadow"

like...

(Some colourful **'like'** comparisons)

all alone like a country dunny

Isolated and lonely as is the outside shithouse.

all dressed up like a pox doctor's clerk

Dressed in cheap and gaudy clothes.

all over her like a rash
all over him like a cheap suit

Someone paying a lot of attention to another.

all over the place like a mad woman's breakfast

Confused, untidy and lacking direction.

all prick and ribs like a drover's dog

Often a description of a lean country lad.

built like a brick shithouse

Men or women of very sturdy build.

carries on like he's got boils on his arse
carries on like a fart in a bottle

Restless, agitated or just a plain arsehole.

charges like the light brigade

charges like a wounded bull

Excessive charging. Often the restaurant bill.

done like a dinner

One who is very well beaten.

eyes like...

road maps
crushed Jaffas
two burnt holes in a blanket
two piss-holes in the snow

The way eyes look after a night on the piss.

fits like a bum in a bucket

Snug.

flat out like a lizard drinking

Extremely busy at work.

getting on like a house on fire

Enjoying another's company.

in and out like a fiddler's elbow

Describes a person of variable moods
but can have a sexual connotation.

in like Flynn

To seize an opportunity - business or sexual.
From the noted sexual prowess of Australian-born actor, Errol Flynn.

lies like a pig in shit

One who is comfortable with deceit.

like a bull at a gate
Impatient and somewhat reckless behaviour.

like shit off a warm shovel
like a shower of shit
like a bat out of hell
like the clappers
like a rat up a drain/rope
like a scalded cat
like the power of piss
like a dose of salts
Moving very quickly and efficiently.

like a bear with a sore head
Bad-tempered.

like a bee in a bottle
Very busy.

like a bump on a log
Out of place, superfluous.
'I was standing there like a bump on a log.'

like a condom filled with walnuts
Description of a well-muscled man.
In the stomach area, it's called a six-pack.

like a dog's breakfast
Very messy.

like a blue-arsed fly

like a dog on lino (linoleum)

Someone moving erratically.

like a fish out of water

like a moll at a christening

like a spare prick at a wedding

like a stunned mullet

Uncomfortable, ill at ease, distracted or unwanted.

like a rat with a gold tooth

One who is insincere and not to be trusted.

like a red rag to a bull

Anything which excites anger.

like a school at Christmas

No class.

like a tin/can of worms

Behaving in an agitated manner.

like a ton of bricks

With great force
- 'the boss came down on me like
a ton of bricks.'

like death warmed up

Someone looking very crook.

like getting blood out of a stone

A near impossible task.

like having a shower with a raincoat on
A man's view of having to wear a condom.

like kissing your sister
There's not a lot in it.

like putting Dracula in charge of the blood bank
like putting Martin Bryant in charge of the gun shop
Not recommended.

like putting marshmallow into a money box
The difficulty of putting a less than erect penis into a tight vagina.

like two ferrets/cats fighting in a sack
like two basketballs in a string bag
like two little boys fighting under a blanket
Descriptions of a woman's ample rear end.

like watching the grass grow
like watching the paint dry
A very slow and boring spectacle.

like water off a duck's back
Having little or no effect.

looks like a drowned rat
Wet and bedraggled.

looks like he just crawled out from under a rock
looks like death warmed up
looks like something the cat dragged in
Looks a sorry sight.

looks like a baby's arm hanging out of a pram holding an apple
An above-average sized penis.

ran like a hairy goat
A punter's description of a losing horse.

running around like a blue-arsed fly
Running around frantically but getting nowhere.

she bangs like a dunny door in a gale
she goes off like a bucket of prawns in the sun
she roots like a rattlesnake
Male comments on a female's sexuality.
Not always based on first-hand knowledge.

shoot through like a Bondi tram
To leave the scene quickly.

squeal like a stuck pig
To protest loudly.

sticks like shit to a blanket
hangs around like a bad smell
Someone who just won't go away.

stood out like a bandicoot on a burnt ridge
stood out like a cocktail bar in the Sahara
stood out like dogs' balls
stood out like a shag on a rock
Very visible.

talks like he's got a mouth full of marbles

Incoherent.

up and down like a bride's nightie
up and down like a honeymoon cock
up and down like a yo-yo

A person of wildly fluctuating emotions.

up her like a rat up a drainpipe
wham-bam-thank-you –ma-am

Fast and opportunistic sex.

went down like a lead balloon

A very unsuccessful result.

I got out of the **roses**, leapt into the **Thyrone**, put on the **bag of fruit** and the **Nazi spy** and took the **bread and jam** down the **frog and toad** to meet a **China** at the **rubbity**.

Had a few **lillies** and before getting too **Adrian**, I decided to nip down to the **J Arthur** for some **Oscar** and then get a **smash and grab** to the **airs and graces.**

I **cast a net** on the **Nelson** but my **condiments and sauces** were too slow and I lost my **sausage and mash**…just couldn't back a **baked dinner**. All I had left was a few **Oxfords** and a little **Kembla** and nobody would take a **Gregory**.

I decided to nip into the **near and far** for a **Ray Stehr** and thought about what I'd tell the **cheese and kisses** who was at home on her **Pat Malone** wondering how she'd pay the **Duke of Kent**.

I went to the **Gene** for a quick **werris** then caught a **left jab** downtown to get some **Arthur Murray** and a bottle of **Lindsay**.

When I got home, the **trouble and strife** had the **Edgars**. She belted me in the **orchestras** before giving me the **Khyber**.

Now I'm out in the **soldiers** feeling very **butchers** after a couple of **up and unders**.

Confused? The answers are here.

Aussie Rhyming SLANG

"Have a Captain Cook
at these"

Originally made popular by the **quick-witted** Cockneys in London's East End, rhyming slang travelled easily to **Australia**, where it was readily adopted and made a part of our culture.

Whilst **rhyming slang** tended to be used mostly in the bush and by the pub, club, and **racecourse** crowd, it also became **popular** with a broader public particularly when a substitute was required for a more direct and perhaps **socially unacceptable** word.

Many original **Cockney words** are still in use in Australia. Many were modified to suit our conditions and others are quintessentially Australian.

Most **rhyming slang** words deal with everyday matters and despite a preoccupation with **drinking, gambling, body parts** and **fornication**, the language is essentially good-natured.

Many rhyming slang words are euphemisms - **Bengal Lancer** (cancer), **Edgar Britt** (shit), **Khyber Pass** (arse).

Some imported words were used during wars and the **Depression** and fell into disuse. Others are very recent and are often based on high-profile **politicians**, **sportsmen** and film and media **identities**.

Rhyming slang has its **rules**. It consists of two or more words the last of which rhymes with the word replaced. Where possible, the shedding of the second or rhyming word is encouraged.

alone — **Pat Malone** (Pat)
Todd Malone (Todd)
'I'm on my Pat (Todd) tonight.'

arms — **Warwick Farm(s)** (warwicks)
Usually refers to lack of underarm hygiene. Someone may be a 'bit woofy' (smelly) or 'Long Jetty' (sweaty) under the Warwicks.
Warwick Farm is a Sydney racecourse.

arse (bum) — **Khyber Pass** (Khyber)
Refers to the anus itself rather than effrontery (more arse than Jessie)
luck (you arsey bastard)
job dismissal (I got the arse)
or sexual achievement (a piece of arse)
For one to tell another to 'stick it up your Khyber' indicates a distinct lack of goodwill between the two.
The pass linking Afghanistan and Pakistan.
Tijuana Brass (Tijuana)
Bulli Pass (Bulli)
Chaminda Vaas
Sri Lankan cricketer.

back — **hammer and tack** (hammer)
To be on someone's hammer is to pursue that person by keeping on his track or figuratively, 'back'. Also used to indicate a sudden lack of employment. 'I got the hammer'. (sack)
Gary Jack
Australian rugby league player.

balls (testicles)
orchestra stalls (orchestras)
Niagara Falls (Niagaras)
town halls
Gladstone Small(s) (Gladstones)
English cricketer.

bank
J. Arthur Rank (J. Arthur)
Used literally - 'I'm going to the J. Arthur' or figuratively by punters - 'I'll put that (winnings) in the J. Arthur.'
UK film producer.
iron tank

bar (hotel)
near and far
'I'll meet you in the near and far.'
Glen McGrath
Australian cricketer.

barber
Sydney Harbour

bed
roses red (roses)
Bill and Ted
Roberta Flack = sack (Roberta)

beer
Ray Stehr
Australian rugby league player.
Terry Dear
Australian radio personality.
pig's ear
Richard Gere
Hollywood actor.

beers
Britney Spears
US singer.

belly	**Ned Kelly** *Notorious Australian bushranger (1857-1880)*
bet (to have a)	**cast a net**
bill (account)	**Jack and Jill** What you get at the end of a restaurant meal.
blonde	**magic wand** As in 'good sort.'
bog (defecate)	**hollow log** One takes a bog as opposed to leaving it. **Rodney Hogg** (Rodney) *Australian cricketer.*
boots	**daisy roots**
booze	**La Perouse** (Larpa) To be, or plan to be 'on the Larpa' suggests rather more than a quiet social drink. *A Sydney suburb.*
boss	**pitch and toss** Of shearing shed origins but now used to describe authority in the workplace.
bowl (cricket)	**Nat King Cole** *US singer.*
bowler (cricket)	**Coca-Cola**

bowlers (lawn) — **rock and rollers**
A somewhat facetious but not unkind term for the mostly elderly folk who play lawn bowls.

brandy — **Fine and Dandy**
Champion Australian racehorse.

bread — **lump of lead**

broke — **hearts of oak**
Often describes lack of success at the racetrack.

brolly (umbrella)	**Aunt Molly**
bum	**deaf and dumb**
bus	**Uncle Gus**
butter	**kerb and gutter**
cab (taxi)	**Sandy McNabb** (Sandy) **left jab** **smash and grab**
can (beer)	**Neville Wran** (Neville) *NSW premier 1976-1986.*
cancer	**Bengal Lancer** **civil answer** **Jack dancer** **Spanish dancer**
cash	**sausage and mash** (sausage) **Oscar Asche** (Oscar) *Aussie actor. (1871-1936)*
chair	**Fred Astair** *Hollywood actor/dancer.*
change (money)	**Kembla Grange** (Kembla) 'Keep the Kembla.' *A racetrack south of Sydney.* **Curtis Strange** *US golfer.*

cheque	**goose's neck** (goose's) **Gregory Peck** (Gregory) **nervous wreck** (nervous)
chest	**George Best** *English football player.*
chilly	**Picadilly**
chunder (vomit)	**up and under** The chunder, or technicolour yawn, has become an Australian institution. Chunders are always colourful.
clock	**dickory dock**
cobber (mate)	**thief and robber**
cock (penis)	**eight day clock** (eight day) The popular clock, which lasted for eight days when fully-wound, somehow contrasts with the average male appendage. **hickory-dickory-dock** **Rupert Murdoch** (Rupert)
coit (bum)	**Jon Voight**
cold	**soldiers bold** (soldiers)
cook	**babbling brook** (babbler) Army and outback cooks not noted for their culinary skills. Also 'crook.' 'I'm feeling a bit babbling brook.'

cop (policeman) — **John Hop**

corner — **Johnny Horner**

crap (shit) — **Andy Capp**

crook (unwell) — **butcher's hook** (butchers)
'I'm feeling a bit butchers.'
Sometimes used for 'look' as in 'have a butchers at this.'

cunt — **drop kick and punt** (drop kick)
Used by one man to describe another man, rather than reference to a woman's anatomy. When one refers to another as a 'drop kick' there is obviously a serious level of animosity between the two.
'All quiet on the Western Front' (all quiet)
Ballina Punt (Ballina)
grumble and grunt
Rex Hunt (Rex)
TV personality.

curry — **Arthur Murray**
When Indian restaurants were changing Australia's eating habits, Arthur Murray was teaching us to dance.

dance — **Jack Palance**
US film actor.

daughter — **ten furlongs = mile-and-a-quarter**

dish — **Lillian Gish**

dole — **rock and roll**
The curious custom of being paid for not working
- 'he's on the rock and roll.'

dollar — **Oxford scholar** (Oxford)
Rhodes scholar

dope (drug) — **Bob Hope**
A broad term for all illegal drugs.

double (racing) — **froth and bubble**

drama — **Vasco de Gama** (no Vasco's)

drink — **cufflink**
Colonel Clink

drugs — **Persian rugs**

drum (racing tip) — **deaf and dumb**

drunk — **elephant's trunk** (elephants)
Being 'elephants' is more socially acceptable than being drunk.
Wally the monk

dunny — **Gene Tunny** (Gene)
The classic Australian outhouse.
US heavyweight boxer.

ears — **ginger beers**
Germaine Greers
Australian feminist.

erection — **state election**
'I feel a state election coming on.'

eyes — **meat/mince pies**
Nelly Blighs
Shane Dyes
Australian jockey.

face — **Martin Place**
boat race
Chevy Chase

fart — **horse and cart**
'Who horse and carted?'

fat (erection) — **Jack Sprat**
larrikin's hat (larrikin)
'I've got half a larrikin.'
Ballarat
Yasser Arafat (Yasser)

feet — **plates of meat**

ferry — **Chuck Berry**
As seen on Sydney Harbour.

finger — **Onkaparinga**
Engagements are formalised by placing the Frank Thring (ring) on the Onkaparinga.
South Australian blanket manufacturer.

fingers — **Mal Meningas**
Rugby league player.

fiver (five dollars) — **Stuart Diver**
Thredbo hero.

flowers — **Cobar showers**

flu
(influenza) — **Dan McGrew**

flush
(poker) — **barmaid's blush**

food — **Rodney Rude** (Rodney)
Australian comedian.

fork — **Duke of York**

fridge
(refrigerator) — **Brooklyn Bridge**

fuck — **Donald Duck** (Donald)
'Did you get a Donald?'
Friar Tuck
rub and tuck

full
(drunk) — **Roy Bull**
'I got a bit Roy Bull last night.'
Rugby league player.

function — **Bondi Junction**
Sydney's best known suburb.

gay
(homosexual) — **Doris Day** (Doris)
Hollywood actor.

gin — **Vera Lynn** (Vera)
Wartime English singer.
Huckleberry Finn (Huckleberry)

gin & water **mile-and-a-quarter**

girl **twist and twirl**

glass (beer) **forward pass**

gloves **turtle doves**

Greek **bubble and squeak**
Werris Creek
Can be used for 'leak' - urinate.

grouse (good) **Mickey Mouse**
In Aussie-speak, grouse means good and extra grouse means very good. Whilst grouse is rarely used today, Mickey Mouse remains. A Mickey Mouse result is a good result, although it can sometimes mean inferior quality - 'a Mickey Mouse watch.'

guts **comic cuts** (comics)
'He hit him in the comics.'

hair **Fred Astair**
American actor/dancer born Fredrick Austerlitz (1899-1987)

hands **German bands**
Ray Millands
Rio Grandes
John Sands
Australian Publishing Company.

harlot **apple charlotte**

hat	**tit for tat** (titfer)
head	**Kelly Ned** **load of bread**
heart	**jam tart** **raspberry tart**
horn (erection)	**early morn** Most erections occur in the early morn. **Sarah Vaughan** (Sarah) *US jazz singer.*
horses (races)	**tomato sauces**
jaw	**Mark McGaw** *Australian rugby league player.*
Jew	**four by two** (fourby) Usually spoken about Jewish people, not to them.
jewellery	**tomfoolery** (tom)
keg (beer)	**Jersey Flegg** *Australian rugby league player.*
kids	**billy lids** (billys) **tin lids** An affectionate term for one's own or somebody else's children.
knackers (balls)	**Jatz crackers** *An Aussie biscuit.*

knees — **gum trees**
Gypsy Rose Lee(s)

lair
(a dandy) — **teddy bear**
One, who by showy dress or ostentatious manner, achieves general contempt.

lay
(sexual intercourse) — **Johnny Ray**
US singer.

leak
(urinate) — **Werris Creek** (werris)
To 'have a werris' is classic Australian rhyming slang for urinating.
A town in NSW.

legs — **bacon and eggs**
fried eggs
Ginger Meggs
Neville Beggs

lie — **pork pie** (porky)
Politicians are good at telling porkies.

lift
(car ride) — **Malcolm Clift** (Malcolm)
Australian rugby league player and coach.

look — **Captain Cook** (captain)
The original Cockney for 'look' was 'butcher's hook.' Now, 'have a captain at this' is the common term.
English explorer/navigator who discovered the east coast of Australia. (1728-1779)

matches — **Jack Scratches**

mate (friend)	**China plate** (China) The common form is China which is so often abbreviated that most are unaware that 'plate' is attached. Used widely by Australian males even though no evidence of real mateship exists.
meal	**Leonard Teal** (Leonard) *Australian actor.*
milk	**Acker Bilk** (Acker) *English jazz musician.*
missus (wife)	**cheese and kisses** (cheese) She who must be obeyed.
money	**Bugs Bunny** **bread and honey**
mouth	**north and south** Pronounced 'norf an souf.'
no dramas	**no Vaso's** Vasco de Gama.
nod	**Murray cod** Refers to betting on credit or 'on the nod.' *An Australian inland river fish.* **Cape Cod**
nose	**I suppose** Queensland shearing shed origins where it applied to a sheep's nose. **Lionel Rose** *Australian boxer.*

nude	**Rodney Rude** *Australian comedian.*
party	**gay and hearty** 'We're having a gay and hearty next week.'
pecker (penis)	**Boris Becker** *A German tennis player of some note.*
pee	**you and me** 'I'm going for a you and me.'
perve (lecherous look)	**hit and swerve** **optic nerve** (optic) The careful study of attractive young ladies. 'Have an optic at that!'
pictures (cinema)	**flea and itches** Classic 1930's RS. People caught the **'bread and jam'** (tram) to the **'flea and itches.'** The term was very appropriate to many of the picture theatres of the time.
piddle	**Nelson Riddle** (Nelson) *US bandleader.* **hi diddle diddle** (hi diddle) **Jimmy Riddle** (Jimmy)
pie (meat)	**dog's eye**
piles	**farmer Giles** **nautical miles** (nauticals)

piss — **hit and miss**
This is the most popular term for this most popular subject.
angel's kiss (angel's)
Johnny Bliss (Johnny)
Australian rugby league footballer.
gypsy's kiss (gypsy's)
snake's hiss (snakes)
Shirley Bliss (Shirley)
Ex-Miss Australia.

pissed — **Adrian Quist** (Adrian)
To some, being 'Mozart', 'Brahms', or 'Schindlers', more accurately describes the state of inebriation. Most RS users however prefer to be 'a bit Adrian.'
Australian tennis player.
Mozart and Liszt (Mozart)
An unlikely alliance of the 18th century Austrian composer Wolfgang Amadeus Mozart and the 19th century Hungarian Franz Liszt.
Schindler's List (Shindlers)
A Hollywood movie based on Thomas Keneally's book, Schindler's Ark.

plate — **Reg Date**
Early Australian soccer player.

pocket — **sky rocket**

pom (pommie) — **to and from**

poof (homosexual) — **horse's hoof** (horses)

poofter — **woolly woofter**

poor — **Archie Moore** (Archie)
Describes a temporary shortage of funds rather than a permanent state of poverty.
US heavyweight boxer.

port (wine) — **Goldsborough Mort**
Early Sydney trading company.

price — **curry and rice**
When asking the price of an item, Australians often use the term 'emmachisit?'

pub (hotel) — **rubbity dub** (rubbity)

pull (masturbate) — **Roy Bull**
Australian rugby league player.
woolly bull

punch — **cut lunch**

queen (homosexual) — **pork and bean**

quinella (horseracing) — **Nelson Mandela** (Nelson)

races (horse) — **airs and graces**

rain — **Frankie Laine**
US singer.

razor — **Dawn Fraser**
Champion Australian swimmer.

rent	**Duke of Kent**
ring	**Frank Thring** *Australian actor.*
river	**shake and shiver**
road	**frog and toad** (frog) To 'hit the frog' is one of the most popular of all RS phrases. **Lew Hoad** *Australian tennis player.*
root (intercourse)	**Angus & Coote** (downtown jeweller) The getting of a 'downtown jeweller' was long a sexual boast of young Sydney men. *A Sydney jewellery firm.* **Ron Coote** (Ronny) *Australian rugby league player.* **Wellington boot** (Wellington)
rum	**dad and mum**
sack (bed)	**hammer and tack** (hammer) Also means dismissal - 'I got the hammer!'
salt	**Harold Holt** *Ex-Australian prime minister.*
sauce (tomato)	**dead horse**
set (tits)	**each way bet**
settle (a bet)	**copper kettle**

sex	**Vincent's and Bex** Old Aussie headache powders.
schooner (beer glass)	**Lilly of Laguna** (Lilly) **Nathan Spooner** (Nathan) *Australian rugby player.*
scotch (whisky)	**Gordon & Gotch** (G & G)
scotch & water	**Gordon and ten** Derives from Gordon & Gotch (scotch) and ten (furlongs) = mile-and-a-quarter = water.
shakes	**Joe Blakes** Usually the aftermath of a serious drinking session.
shark	**Noah's Ark** (Noah)
sharks	**after darks**
shave	**Dad and Dave** *Popular pre-war radio serial of the same name.*
sheep	**willow the weep** *An Aussie shearing shed term.*
sheila (woman)	**Charlie Wheeler** (Charlie) Women today prefer not to be called sheilas or charlies. **Bulahdelah** *NSW town.*

shirt — **Ernie and Bert**

shit — **Edgar Britt** (Edgar)
Refers to the function rather than the end-product. One goes for an Edgar.
Famous Aussie jockey.
Jimmy Britt (boxer)
hard hit

shits — **tom tits**
Emotional rather than physical.
One gives another the tom tits.

shivers — **Hawkesbury Rivers** (Hawkesburys)
A convenient rhyme despite the fact that there is only one Hawkesbury River.
A river north of Sydney.

shocker — **Barry Crocker** (Barry)
Usually refers to a sportsman having a bad game.
Aussie actor famous for his Bazza McKenzie *role.*

shoes — **St Louis Blues** (St Louies)
Basin Street Blues (Basin Streets)
Merv Hughes
Australian cricketer.

short (of money) — **Holmes á Court**
Being short of money was an experience unknown to the late Australian business tycoon, Robert Holmes á Court.

shout (bar) — **Wally Grout** (Wally)
When it's your 'Wally' it's your turn to buy the next round of drinks.
Aussie Test cricketer of the 60's.
'It's your hook' (your turn to buy)

shower — **Tyrone Power** (Tyrone)
Hollywood actor.

sick — **Tom and Dick**

silly — **Uncle Willy**
'Don't be Uncle Willy.'

sin — **Vicker's Gin**

sister — **skin and blister**

six (cricket) — **Tom Mix**

skin — **thick and thin**

slang — **Jack Lang**
Ex-premier of NSW.

sleep — **bo peep**

slut — **mud hut**

smoke (cigarette) — **laugh and joke**

snake — **Joe Blake**

snooze — **Tom Cruise**
Hollywood actor.

soap — **Cape of Good Hope**

socket (golf) — **Davy Crockett**
The fear of all golfers.

socks — **Joe Rocks**
almond rocks (almonds)

soup — **loop-the-loop**

speech — **Bill Peach**
One may be called upon to make a Bill Peach at the next Bondi Junction (function).
Aussie TV personality.

stairs — **apples and pears**

steak — **off-break**
Cricketing term.

stork (penis) — **Belle of New York**

story — **john dory** (JD)
'What's the JD?' - 'what's happening?'
An Aussie coastal fish.

suit — **bag of fruit**

sweaty — **Long Jetty**
A NSW town.

swim — **Tiger Tim**

Sydney — **steak and kidney**

table — **Clark Gable**
Hollywood actor.

taxi — **Joe Maxie**
Fred and Maxie

tea — **you and me**
'Let's have a cup of you and me.'

teeth — **Ted Heath**
Ex-*English prime minister.*
Barrier Reef (Barriers)

telephone — **Al Capone**
This popular term immortalises the Italian-born Chicago crime boss who somehow managed to die of natural causes in 1947.
dog and bone
eau-de-cologne

tenner *(ten dollars)* — **Ayton senna**

thief — **tea leaf**
Applies to those engaged in petty theft rather than serious crime.

tie — **Nazi spy**
2KY
Sydney radio station.

time — **Harry Lime**
Of the film 'Third Man' fame.
'What's the Harry Lime?'

tip (racing) — **egg flip**

tits — **brace and bits**
threepenny bits (threepennies)
Brad Pitts
Eartha Kitts
each way bet = set.

titties — **Bristol Cities** (Bristols)
Original Cockney. The most popular term for this most popular subject.
Salt Lake Cities (Salt Lakes)
Vatican Cities (Vaticans)

toes — **these and those**

tool (penis) — **April fool**

toss (cricket) — **Joe Loss**
English bandleader.

tote (totalisator) — **giddy goat/nanny goat**

towel — **Baden Powell**
Lord Baden Powell (1857-1941).
Founder of the Boy Scouts movement.

tram — **bread and jam**

trots (harness racing) — **dry rots**
red hots
Early harness racing was notorious for 'arranged' race results.
Red hot is slang for crooked.

trouble — **Barney Rubble** (Barney)

trousers — **council houses**

try (rugby) — **meat pie**

tub (bath) — **Bib and Bub**

turd — **Henry the Third** (Henry)
Describes the tangible result of defecation as well as being a derogatory and very unkind description of another.
King of England (1216-1272)

turner (cricket) — **bunsen burner**
A cricketing term for a wicket which is taking spin.

tyke (Roman Catholic) — **marlin spike**

uncle — **Simon and Garfunkel**

undies (underwear) — **Reg Grundys**
Aussie TV identity.

waiter — **hot potato**
Pronounce potato as 'potatah' and the sense is maintained.

wank (masturbate) — **walk the plank**

wanker — **merchant banker**
The term wanker was originally used to describe those who were perceived to be regularly engaged in masturbation. Now used in a broader sense to identify those whose behaviour is unusual, unpleasant or generally unacceptable.

wash — **lemon squash**

water — **squatter's daughter**

wave (ocean) — **Indian brave**

whisky — **gay and frisky**

wicket (cricket)	**Wilson Pickett**
wide (cricket)	**Frank Hyde** *Aussie rugby league player and commentator.*
wife	**trouble and strife** (trouble)
wig	**Moreton Bay fig** (Moreton Bay) **syrup fig** (syrup)
wine	**Lindsay Kline** (Lindsay) *Australian cricketer of the 60's.*
winner	**baked dinner** Punters seek a 'baked dinner' more than they seek a baked dinner.
wog	**Dapto Dog** (Dapto) During WW2, 'wog' was a common and not unkind description of those of Middle Eastern origin. Today it is seen as racist and usage is not recommended.
worries	**River Murrays** (rivers) Usually abbreviated to 'rivers' as in 'no rivers.' Also 'no wucking furries.'
Yank	**septic tank** (septic) (seppo) A somewhat unfortunate but essentially good-natured reference to Americans. An *upmarket dunny.*

"Well, I'll be blowed!"

"owyagoin
champ?"
FORM

Old Aussie expressions

Words, phrases and expressions, which were once popular but are mostly used today in the bush or by those who are old enough to remember.

ace it up!
turn it up! Stop it!

alive and kicking
Someone very much alive and well.

all dolled-up/ponced-up
Dressed in one's best.

bags To claim a place - 'I bags being first.'

beaudy! Something exceptional - 'It's a real beaudy!'
Pleasant surprise - 'you bloody beaudy!'

beg yours? I beg your pardon?

billyo To go far away or to go quickly
- 'he went to billyo.'
Or 'he went like billyo.'

bloody oath! An emphatic yes
- 'am I going to the pub? Bloody oath I am!'

blow me down!
Exclamation of amazement,
surprise or disbelief.

blow through To leave. Often to leave in a hurry so as to avoid one's responsibilities.

blowed! **Be blowed!** - no, get lost!
I'll be blowed! - surprise.
Blowed if I know! - I don't know.

bluey Curiously, this describes a red-haired man.

blurb Usually unwanted advertising material.

bobby-dazzler Someone (or something) which is very good or exceptional
- 'his girlfriend is a real bobby-dazzler.'

bodgie A young man of the 50's who dressed in a very flamboyant style.
Also describes an inferior product
- 'that was a bodgie car you sold me.'

bonzer Excellent and deserving of admiration
- 'he's a bonzer bloke.'

boo-boo A mistake - 'he made a real boo-boo.'

bottler Something or someone of exceptional quality
- 'he's a real bottler.'

break it down!
fair crack of the whip!
Be reasonable - give me a fair go.

brushback A hairstyle. In the 50's, many smart young men did the brushback.

bullamakanka
Any remote place in the outback - somewhere near the '**black stump**' or '**woop woop**.'

bully for you!
A sarcastic exclamation of envy or contempt.

bumfluff The first growth of a young man's facial hair.

bumper A half smoked cigarette.
Many Aussie urinals have signs reading:
- 'please don't discard your bumpers here.
It makes them soggy and hard to light.'

bung on side
Pompous and overbearing behaviour.

burl To have a go - 'let's give it a burl.'

bush week 'What do you think it is - bush week?'
An answer given to a stupid question.

cat's pyjamas
Someone who thinks he's the cat's pyjamas or the cat's whiskers, is conceited or largely up himself.

champion A friendly greeting - 'owyagoin champion?'

chap Man. 'He's not a bad chap.'

charlie A woman.

chin wag A chat - 'I ran into Charlie the other day and we had a real good chin wag.'

cobber A good friend.

codger An old man.
'What happened to that old codger?'

coot Same as a codger but a lot less respectful.

cove Man. 'He's not a bad cove.'

chucker-outer
A pub or nightclub bouncer who is usually built like a brick shithouse and who evicts troublemakers.

clobber Clothes - 'put on your good clobber.'
Also to bash someone - 'I clobbered him.'

cock-eyed Something which is unbalanced or irregular - 'that building's a bit cock-eyed.'
The origin of the word is therefore obvious.

come off the grass!
Exclamation of disbelief.

comeuppance
Just reward for bad behaviour - 'he'll get his comeuppance.'

cossie Swimming costume.
Also trunks, bathers or togs.

crack Male and female fundamental orifices.

crikey!/cripes!
Expressions of astonishment.

cropper To fall heavily - 'he got pissed and came a cropper.'

curl the mo! An expression of wonder, amazement, admiration or pleasure.

dead marine An empty beer bottle.

dekko A look - 'have a dekko at this.'

diddle To cheat - 'he diddled me.'

dinger Bum - 'I'll kick him up the dinger.'

dinky-di If you're dinki-di or dinkum, you're straightforward and truthful.

dirty big Very large.

dish up Mum always announced that the meal was about to be dished up - served.

do A function -'we're going to a do at the club.'

do a bunk To run away from one's commitments or 'blow through.'

do a line To 'do a line' is to flirt with a woman in order to achieve short or long-term goals.

do your dough
To lose your money.

dooks Hands - 'put up your dooks and fight.'

dough **moolah/spondulicks**
Money.

dribs and drabs
Small and irregular amounts - 'the party guests arrived in dribs and drabs.'

drongo Dull-witted and stupid person.

fair crack of the whip!
fair suck of the sav!
Plea for fair treatment.

fanny In Australian, it means a woman's private parts. In America, it means a woman's rear end.

flaming Euphemism for bloody or damned - 'he's a flaming idiot.'

flash Flamboyant, showy, ostentatious - a flash car.

flea house The local picture theatre.

flicks Movies. You used to see the flicks in the flea house.

flip Someone just short of a boof head - 'he's a flip.'

for crying out loud
A plea for fair play.

forklift The pillows on the back seat of early Holdens.

frig around To behave foolishly - waste time - 'he's always frigging around.' Euphemism for that other …ing word.

galoot A stupid person.

gargle A drink - 'let's go down to the pub for a gargle.'

geek A look - 'have a geek at this.'

gee whiz! An expression of surprise.

geezer Usually an older man - 'that old geezer.'

get a wriggle on!
Get moving!

gift of the gab
A glib speaker is said to have the gift of the gab.

give it a whirl
To make an attempt - 'I'll give it a whirl.'

gizmo A convenient word for anything - 'hand me that gizmo.'

go crook To complain strongly about something - 'I'm going to go crook about this.'

go you halves
To split the bet and the winnings with someone - 'I'll go you halves.'

gob Mouth - 'shut your gob.'

golly A large and usually well-formed mass of phlegm which is projected from the mouth with considerable speed and accuracy by those given to this unfortunate practice.

goolie A stone - 'he chucked a goolie.'

guzzle Serious drinking without much concern for the niceties.

hairy goat A very slow racehorse - 'the bloody thing ran like a hairy goat.'

heck! Exclamation of annoyance or frustration.

hobnob To mix with a crowd for potential gain - 'he's always hobnobbing with that rich crowd.'

hoo-roo Good-bye. See you later. Sometimes **'hoo-ray,' ta ta.**

horn An erection. The aim was and still is to crack a horn.

hubby Husband.

hullabaloo A commotion or disruption. 'Everybody got drunk and it was a real hullabaloo.'

humdinger Exceptionally good - 'he's a real humdinger.'

hunky-dory In good order - 'everything's hunky dory.'

in a jiffy/tick In very short time - 'I'll be there in a tick.'

in fits and starts Irregularly.

in the good books In favour - 'I'm in the good books at home.'

jake Everything's all right - 'she'll be jake.'

job To hit or bash someone - 'I jobbed him.'

joker An Aussie bloke. Usually 'an old joker.'

kafuffle An argument, commotion or fight.

kitty A common fund of money - 'we'll put the winnings in the kitty.'

knock your block off
A serious physical threat.

kybosh To put an end to something - 'he put the kybosh on that deal.'

long in the tooth
Someone who is old or is seen to be old - 'he's a bit long in the tooth.'

make it snappy!
Be quick!

my oath! Emphatic agreement - 'my oath I will.'

makings The materials required for the rolling of one's own cigarettes. Tobacco and papers. 'Have you got the makings?'

molly-dooker
A left-handed person.
Also **'southpaw'** or **'leftie.'**

month of Sundays
A long time
- 'I haven't seen him for a month of Sundays.'

muck-about
To do nothing in particular or bugger-all.

nippy Refers to a drop in the temperature
- 'it's a bit nippy this morning.'
Also used to describe people very quick on their feet - 'he's a nippy little player.'

okey dokey OK, approval, acceptance.

one-armed bandit
The old-style poker machine operated by a side lever.

other-half Wife or husband
- 'I'll check with the other/better half.'

peanut gallery
The cheap seats at the picture theatre where people were usually noisy. Thus, 'quiet in the peanut gallery!'

piddle To urinate - 'I need a piddle.'
Or 'who piddled on the floor?'

piker A person who backs out of a deal.

plonk A general term for wine before table wine became fashionable.

P.O.Q. Piss off quick.

pull your head in
Just short of saying shut up!

raining cats and dogs
Raining heavily.

right as rain Everything's OK.

ripper Excellent - 'he's a ripper bloke.'

scone The head - 'I hit him on the scone.'

scrub The bush or outback. He's 'up the scrub' or '**gone bush**.' Also to cancel or do away with - 'we scrubbed the idea.'

shank's pony Feet as the means of transport.

sheila Women of all ages - 'a young sheila,' 'an old sheila.'

sherbet A beer - 'we're going down for a few sherbets.'

shiack To play the fool. - 'he was shiacking around.'

shikkered Drunk - 'old Charlie was shikkered again last night.'

shit a brick! An expression of annoyance or frustration. Sometimes 'shit a brick and fart blue sparks!'

sissy An effeminate man.

skerrick Usually applies to lack of food in the house - 'I haven't got a skerrick in the fridge.'

skew-whiff Out of order. In disarray - 'our plans have gone skew-whiff.'

skite A boastful person. Often stated as someone who is up himself or full of shit - 'he's a real skite.'

sly grog Alcohol sold illegally from a sly grog shop.

smithereens Tiny fragments - 'the vase was smashed to smithereens.'

smoko A break from work for a quiet puff of the weed.

snow A blond-haired man.

squiz To look - 'have a squiz at this.'

starve the lizards!
stone the crows!
Exclamations of annoyance or frustration.

stingy Mean.

strewth! An expression of surprise or amazement.

strides/tweeds
Men's pants.

strike me dead/lucky/pink/roan!
Expressions of surprise, indignation or frustration.

tassel/tonk/donk
Penis.

the wife A rather chauvinistic way a man introduced or spoke of his wife.

togs Usually a bathing suit, but can refer to clothes.

too right! An emphatic yes.

took a shine
To quickly come to like a relative stranger - 'I really took a shine to him.'

towel up To win comprehensively - 'he really towelled him up.'

troppo Crazy, mad - 'he's gone troppo.'

tucker Food - 'they've got great tucker.'

turn Being somewhat unwell. Elderly relatives always took the occasional 'turn.'

turnout Any sort of a party or function - 'we're going to a turnout on Saturday.'